THE NIGHTS OF LONDON

BY THE SAME AUTHOR

THE HEART OF LONDON
THE SPELL OF LONDON
LONDON (LITTLE GUIDES)
IN SEARCH OF ENGLAND
THE CALL OF ENGLAND
IN SEARCH OF SCOTLAND
IN SEARCH OF IRELAND
IN SEARCH OF WALES
BLUE DAYS AT SEA

THE NIGHTS OF LONDON

BY

H. V. MORTON

SIXTH EDITION

METHUEN & CO. LTD.
36 ESSEX STREET W.C.
LONDON

First Published	. . .	*November 11th*	*1926*
Second Edition	. . .	*May*	*1929*
Third Edition	. . .	*May*	*1930*
Fourth Edition	. . .	*April*	*1931*
Fifth Edition	. . .	*February*	*1932*
Sixth Edition	. . .	*1932*	

PRINTED IN GREAT BRITAIN

To
MIDSUMMER NIGHT

Contents

The full streets beckon : Come, for toil has burst his bars,
And idle eyes rejoice, and feet unhasting go.
O let us out and wander the gay and golden night.

—LAURENCE BINYON, 'London Visions'

THE NIGHTS OF LONDON

NIGHT in London.

We are off again on more adventures. Before us lies the mystery of dark London, of London under the glow of lamps; London under moon and stars; London under fretful, dull skies. Before us, also, lies danger—the awful danger of repeating a story that has been well told already. You must leave this to me and hope for the best. I promise not to drag you through that inevitable night on the Thames Embankment or the equally ancient night in a doss-house. I will try to take you as little as I must in the well-worn footsteps of other night-errants. I may not do half so well. I do not know; for the night of London is a dark puzzle in which it is possible to find almost anything.

When night falls over London ancient and primitive things come to our streets; for night is sinister, dramatic; it brings with it something of the jungle. Beasts of prey and great cities alone in nature remain awake when darkness comes; the one in search of death, the other in search of an extra hour of life.

The very quality of the darkness in a great city like London is itself a study. The darkness of

Pall Mall is different from the darkness of Bishopsgate; the lights of Piccadilly are different from the lights of the Edgware Road. And the men and women who move slowly through the streets of London at night, complex in motive, freed from work, moving for once at the bidding of their own wills, their faces bloodless in the pale stream of lamplight, gliding past in waves, a concentration of all those unknown things that have made great cities since Babylon a mystery and a heartache.

* * *

No man, I think, can say that the words 'Night in London' leave him entirely unmoved. To the student of human nature they act like a whip on the imagination, for night in London is a brief period of infinite possibility. Dickens placed strange people in strange places, but Stevenson placed strange people in ordinary places, and thus enlarged the possibilities of romance and gave life a new terror—or a new thrill. No matter how often life proves to us that pale ladies in deep sorrow (and limousines) do not glide to the pavement edge and whisper, "Follow this car and save me!" yet at night we are almost persuaded that adventures in which fate has cast us as the hero lie just round the next corner. This rarely happens; but it explains why some people get into trouble at night!

There is in the heart of the darkness an allurement that calls, promising that somewhere in this respite from day is a release from routine, telling us that the world is free to us.

* * *

Night life is the last social habit to be developed by a city. It is only since the growth of the West End, the invention of gas and the establishment of a police force that London has had the opportunity and the audacity to plunge into the night.

Roman London must have been deadly dull after dark; Saxon London duller still. The curfew which announced the official night of Norman London must have acted as a damper on any gaiety that happened to survive the Conquest. The law of the Middle Ages assumed that any man who walked the streets at night was bent on evil (which was probably true); Tudor London developed a little patch of vice and villainy on Bankside, but it is not until the Georgian Age that we observe the first Nights of London. Beyond the walls of the City had grown up the West End with its squares, and it is in this new London that we see for the first time the night hawk sitting behind the yellow windows of St. James's Street staking his estate on a throw of the dice.

I suppose no age devotes itself to nocturnal gaiety till its women dress for dinner. Mrs. Dick Whittington, I feel sure, had no evening gowns. She wore her best gown trimmed with miniver indiscriminately at noon or night; for a 'riding' along Chepe or for a State banquet. In the

Georgian Age, however, white shoulders flashed through the tinted dusk of Ranelagh and Vauxhall. In the new West End the torches of the link men grew pale in the dawn as a tired beauty was borne in her sedan chair from a rout.

The night life of the Georgians was the brilliant effervescence of the privileged few. Behind the wildest party was always the old London problem of getting home, complicated in that age by the solemn thought that Dick Turpin might be waiting with his pistols cocked behind a hedge in Mayfair. Still that did not deter them: our forefathers contrived to have a marvellous time by candle-light. We should feel a kind of reflected glory in gout.

The lights of London grew brighter in the next century till they blazed relentlessly on a boiled shirt in a hansom cab. We are now almost in modern times. The London of the Georgians had been naughty; the London of the staid Victorians became wicked; that, at least, was her reputation; and they say that where smoke is there is generally fire. Night crowds, not made up of lords and ladies but of ordinary Londoners, filled the Strand, for years the most famous street in the world, which handed over its supremacy to Piccadilly almost in our own times and fell into position as a kind of connecting link between the staid old city on the hill and the giddy young West End.

Old men who drink port have told me, when warmed up, how beautiful London was at night in those days of side whiskers and plaid trousers and

Ouida. They have described to me the unforgettable sensation, unknown to this age, of waiting outside a stage door with a bunch of flowers. The Georgian night was sustained by port; the Victorian by champagne: this was the age of Clicquot. A series of sharp explosions and a barrage of corks went up in the Strand restaurants every night as grandfather leaned single-mindedly towards his favourite ballet girl.

Now the nights of London through which we shall journey in the following pages are free to all men. The cheap restaurant, the tube train, the omnibus, have packed the West End at night. The desire to extract just a little more from life than Nature intended, confined during the eighteenth century to the quality and during the nineteenth to the man with money, is now shared by the millions of London. The bright lights call them night after night, if only to saunter for an innocent hour in the slow, exciting crowds.

This, then, is our stage. It is an interesting one. By day we can say that London obeys a master; by night she is her own mistress. She is not bound to stay up after dark; in fact the doctors say that it is very unwise.

* * *

Something more.

Among the eight millions which are London in its Greatness are thousands of men and women who sleep by day and work by night in order that we may eat new bread for breakfast, drink fresh milk, read our newspaper, and be in the position to slip unwelcome letters behind the clock before we begin a new day.

How often do we think of these children of the London night—these work-o'nights—who sleep in hushed homes with blinds closed against the day-light and sally forth at dark to perform work that upholds so much uneasiness in our lives ?

What manner of people are these owls of London, and how do they like living behind the back of the sun ?

I will go through the silent streets of London and discover them to you. I will describe them and their opinions and their tasks ; for these are our companions in London of whom we know little, of whom we think less. . . .

But look, a little half-moon lies over the Thames ! The stage is set. Let us go out into dark streets.

The Dead City

TWO o'clock in the morning at the Bank. . . . Arc lights burn over empty streets. It is so cold, so quiet. The Lord Mayor of London asleep behind the Corinthian columns of his dark, island house ; the lieutenant in charge of the Bank Guard (soothed by traditional port) asleep opposite behind the eyeless frontage of Soane's stone money-box ; the constables of the Royal Exchange asleep in the suburbs, their cocked hats on the bed-posts, their silver, Elizabethan bears above white sheets . . . dreaming of Gloriana, perhaps, who made them, or of scrubby little office boys who live on apples and leave the cores to plague their lives.

This is the Bank : the busiest scene by day in London ; by night the most desolate, most forlorn ! A forest has at night a hidden life ; even the Sahara and the Libyan desert seem to pulse with a queer vitality under the stars, but the City of London, made by man and deserted by its creator, dies each night. Dead as Timgad, it seems ; as uncanny in its shuttered trance as some lost city of old times discovered standing in silence under an indifferent moon.

I stand by the Duke of Wellington, gripped by the silence of this so recently crowded stage, feeling in some small way the horror of being the last man left on earth.

A black tom-cat of great girth and dignity comes

down from Cheapside into Poultry with an air which suggests that he is the managing director of London, Limited. He alone treads roads which a few hours since would have meant annihilation; leisurely he comes, as if savouring the solitude, as if purring in the silence. He stands a moment lost in thought, and then slowly crosses the road—Cheapside to his tail, the Royal Exchange to his whiskers, the Bank to his left, the Mansion House to his right—the only living thing in the core of London's sleeping heart!

In the desolation of the Bank at two a.m. he is an event.

'Puss-puss,' I whisper.

He considers me and rejects me in the manner of cats. What right have I to be messing about in the coverts scaring the quarry? He walks to the Royal Exchange, and is lost round a corner. I wonder whether he will hunt the rat over those stones from Turkey on which London found her fortune.

A taxicab spins across from Queen Victoria Street; one of those curious unbalanced motor-sweepers releases its brushes and hums beside the kerb in Poultry, going slowly on into the lamplit solitude like an ugly garbage beetle.

* * *

I meet a policeman in Cornhill; another one in Gracechurch Street.

London must have felt like this during the Great Plague; these silent locked buildings and these dead avenues! A square mile of solitude where once was such throbbing life, where London behind her wall lived and slept, married, died, and was buried. There can be no such things as ghosts, or the empty City of London would be full of thin, mistlike clouds every night, clouds with faces in them, peering, wondering.

Who could resist going on past the Monument to London Bridge?

London Bridge deserted, twin rows of lamps over the dark river, and—such a heart-catching beauty of London lost in a faint night mist, picked out with pin stars of light, the Thames in movement round the jutting piers, barred with gold fish scales of lamplight, and, to the right, a great splendour of grey spires, and dark stones. . . . London asleep! No sound but that of a stray, petulant siren downstream; no movement in all London but an approaching red tug light on the Thames, the rush of lit water and a sudden puff of steam from the Cannon Street railway bridge; a white cloud lit with red flame for an instant and then lost. . . .

This is the time to see London, to love London, to make promises to London, to pray to London, to plead with London; for London now, grotesquely, seems all yours in loneliness, for once in the twenty-four hours harmless, unable to hurt or bless . . . lost in a dream.

* * *

I go down Lower Thames Street, where the cats

are all in love, sitting crouched low, face to face, whirring inside with savage sonnets, advancing, retreating, eye to eye. I come to the Tower of London, which lifts grey walls and bastions in the night. One small window only is lit; a tiny square of gold high up in a turret. The mind fastens to it. I think of a knight hurriedly arming in the stone room and his horse ready below. . . . I think of a yeoman warder with neuralgia! Such a speculative little window in a London night!

I creep to the wicket gate and peer in at the sleeping Tower of London. A shadow at the gate moves. I see the light run on steel:

'Who goes there?'

The Tower is awake: that is the discovery of a City night! The Tower is as it always was: a fortress locked with a password, locked by the King's keys, slipping back into medievalism every night prompt at ten.

'Who goes there?'

In the voice of the sentry at the wicket gate is the Voice of our London coming down, with a slight touch of indignation, over eight hundred splendid years.

When the 'Tubes' Stop

THE last train had flung its golden chain into the mouth of the tunnel. Piccadilly Station was now closed. The moving staircases were not moving, the lifts were not lifting, the 'Book Here' signs were all lies (for you could not book anywhere): and over the ninety-six miles of tube track was a silence as of death. It was almost one a.m.

I stood in the desolate Piccadilly Circus Station watching a musical cleaner sweep up the litter of a day's tube crowd to the tune of 'Yes, Sir, She's My Baby.' Such a queer litter: reams of silver paper, bits of biscuit, chocolate, cigarette packets, envelopes, the heel of a white satin dance shoe, and —unspeakably disreputable and riotous—an old umbrella that had snapped somewhere. I thought of the things you see on the floor of a monkey's cage in the Zoo! What an unfair reminder of so many thousands of delightful people now in bed. . . .

It was sad and lonely. The advertisements, to my weary, one a.m.-ish eyes, were insolent; the thought of drinking vermouth was in itself intolerable; the idea of spending a holiday in Scotland entirely loathsome.

* * *

Two whistling bill-posters arrived with a ladder,

a bucket, and a roll of paper. They went to the edge of the platform.

'Is the juice off yet, Bill?'

'No,' replied Bill. 'Gimme a fag.'

They waited. A group of workmen carrying leather bags from which protruded the blunt noses of large hammers stood together at the platform's end, their attention divided between the acetylene lamps which they carried and the railway lines. This interest in the lines is characteristic of all who inhabit the tube stations when the last train has gone by. Men look at the rails as a dog looks at a sleeping cat—a will-it-bite expression! A foreman climbed down to the track, fixed a metal shoe to one conductor rail and a thing shaped like a small doll's house to the other. Immediately the doll's house became illuminated by twelve electric bulbs—the juice was still juicy!

He gave a respectful glance at the track and climbed back into safety.

A young man hurried down the platform towards me:

'Good morning!' he said briskly. 'I'm from the engineer's department, and I'm going to take you for a walk through the tunnel to Leicester Square. Shall we get a move on?'

'The—er—juice,' I began thoughtfully, 'is still, apparently, active, and lively. . . .'

'Oh, that's all right,' he said heartily as he leapt down into the death zone. 'So long as you don't fall across the conductor rails, you know. . . .'

I hate being brave; I hate these situations from

which it is not possible to retreat with self-respect. I jumped down beside him and walked on in a manner which would have given Agag, who came unto Samuel 'delicately', a number of most useful hints.

* * *

You may not realize that when the tubes cease work the current is switched off in sections. As each section becomes 'juiceless', gangs of men waiting at the stations set out to examine every yard of the one hundred and seventy-one miles of track on the Tube and District systems. It is probably the most important four hours' work during the London night. Every nut, bolt, screw, lamp, wire, signal, telephone, disk, sleeper, key, and rail is hit and prodded and peered at; they even go over every yard of the great iron ribs of the tunnels. They wander on like explorers in an Egyptian tomb; and this resemblance is intensified by occasional mosquitoes which live in this even temperature all the year long.

I did not see one. I am told, however, that gangers who go to sleep often awaken bitten; but as a stray ganger is the only brightness in the life of a tube mosquito—for they never penetrate to the richer potentialities of the stations—who shall grudge them an infrequent happiness?

We walked on through a gloom lit by small flasks of *crême de menthe*. We came to a straight stretch of track on which the rails converged to a point, and over this track swarmed men with hammers. The tunnel boomed with their knocking.

'The juice is off!' said the engineer, promptly walking on the live rail. I looked at him, silently abhorring the over-confidence of all mechanically minded men. Not to be outdone in courage, I lifted a foot gingerly and gave the rail a coy kick; then, as I still appeared to be in existence, I boldly stepped on it with both feet. Apart from a second in which I experienced all the pangs of electrocution, there was nothing to report except a faint feeling of foolishness to be walking along a thing which any madman breaking into the power station could have filled with death in half a second.

We chatted to the repair gang. We collected one of the oldest night workers in the tube, Mr. Parsons, who waved a white acetylene lamp in our faces and became technical to the engineer.

These men love their tunnels; they take a pride in keeping every nut tight, they tell you in the same tone of voice that men say 'the wife's not very well', that water is still leaking slightly through the iron joints by the 'dead end'.

'What,' I asked Mr. Parsons, 'is the most extraordinary thing you have found in a tube tunnel?'

'A dead 'un,' he replied bluntly.

* * *

Our arrival at Leicester Square was supremely nightmareish.

There stood Leicester Square Station as we all know it: advertisements, clocks, lights, indication boards and—not a soul on it! We limped in a leisurely way, now on the rails, now on the sleepers, talking in loud echoing tones about Mr. Baldwin’s voice as heard over wireless, the prospects of television and the mummy of Tutankhamen. We stood looking at desolate Leicester Square as two archaeologists might regard it in two thousand years, if London, by that time, is lost and ruined. A gang of men emerged from the opposite tunnel with a brazier and many hammers.

They swarmed like rats over the rails.

‘By the way, I have seen no rats,’ I said.

‘There are very few,’ replied the engineer.

‘I suppose this hammering is going on everywhere?’

‘Over one hundred and seventy-one miles of track,’ he said.

* * *

They unlocked Leicester Square for me and I came out under the mild scrutiny of a policeman into cold, empty streets.

Ships at Night

THREEPENCE. I gave it to the conductor at Ludgate Circus and left the omnibus at Limehouse. If I had paid fifty pounds for my ticket I could not have travelled farther from the London that most of us know. The West India Dock Road is as glorified by darkness as the native quarter of an Oriental city; its meanness is swallowed up in shadows; the jutting lamps in dark side lanes leer adventure; the lit windows near the roofs of rickety houses hold a sordid promise of thrill; and I sniffed the air hopefully for the unforgettable pungency of opium, but found only the unforgettable pungency of fish and chips.

The pavements were barred across by light falling from the windows of eating-houses and cook-shops. In these shafts of brilliance Chinamen passed me without 'brushing' past me—as in the best literature—and I wondered as I gazed at their frozen faces and their live slit eyes, like the eyes of animals looking from a cave, whether such masks conceal drama or only mild domesticity down Limey-housey-Causey-way—as they call it.

A lascar shuffled past; a group of three vague Asiatics turned suddenly into a side alley. I wanted to follow, to find out if these stories are true. I had half a mind to break my tryst with the dock police, but, without warning—I came face to face with high spiked gates, and before me lay the docks at night.

* * *

'There's a bit of a river mist,' said the police inspector, handing me an electric torch as we stepped out into pitch blackness.

Now the docks are one of London's great thrills by day, and by night they are one of London's great pictures.

In this lonely land of darkness, full of titanic shadows, where huge ships lift themselves into the night like mountains, you realize the startling variety that one great city can hold. Here is a new London within half an hour of St. Paul's: a London of dramatic gloom, tramping night patrols, shadows like men and men like shadows, the whole place tinged with the grim romance of labour on the Seven Seas, and vivid with the feeling of ships at rest, the water licking at their anchor chains.

We turned a corner of a shed. In the darkness the dock-side cranes stood straddle-legged like queer Martians. Three yellow portholes shone in the side of a large West Indiaman. We stepped over a coil of rope and were talking of something when, suddenly, the inspector stopped in his tracks and flashed a moon of white light into a corner. In this darkness a man stood blinking in the torchlight.

'Hallo, sir!' said the man.

'So it's you, is it?' said the inspector. 'What's up?'

The man gathered himself to tell us what was 'up'; and in this he was entirely successful, for he had developed the gift of fluent expression. His problem was whether the great big blinkin' teak ship would blinkin' well put out at this time of blinkin' night and collide with his blinkin' barge in the fog.

We made reassuring noises, but he was not to be interrupted. It was something he had been saving up all alone in the darkness of the dock, and he was glad to unburden his soul. . . .

It appeared to him that if the blinkin' people responsible for the unloading of London cargoes could blinkin' well tip their ships upside down and empty the stuff on the wharf in five minutes and load them again in five minutes they'd be off again to blinkin' Jamaica before you could say Jack blinkin' Robinson, and, strike him pink. . . .

Before either of us could do this a melancholy 'moo' sounded in the mist: the deep moo of a doubtful siren. It electrified our blinkin' friend. He called on all the deities who safeguard the barges of lightermen and leapt at random into the darkness. . . .

* * *

The millions of pounds' worth of goods which the world sends to the Port of London are guarded through the night by young men in blue who have a nasty habit of looking like the end of a shed and suddenly stepping out with an 'All correct, sir!' to their inspector. They step back and melt into the shed again.

'All the rum that enters England comes here,' said the inspector, flashing his torch on an army of vast barrels lying stacked in rows.

'Thirty over proof,' we read on them.

'We can store four million gallons of it,' he said. To a sailor this must be one of the most impressive spots on earth.

* * *

'There's precious little thieving in the docks these days,' said the inspector. 'We know every hole and corner of them. It may seem impossible to you, but we know every coil of rope and every brick that's left lying about. The river "rats" who used to pilfer have turned their attention to stuff lying out on the Thames, and the Thames police are kept busy with them. We don't often get a thief here.

'It's a funny thing the way people give Limehouse and Wapping a bad name. I suppose it's the writers that do it. You've no idea how mild and quiet people are down here, except for an occasional scrap when the pubs close. I know a pal who married a girl from Brixton, and when she had to come and live at Wapping—oh, my, wasn't there a business! She thought—well, I don't know what she didn't think. But she goes about at all hours of the day and night, and nicer, better-mannered people she says she never met—even in

Brixton! She's a good deal safer from being insulted than she would be in the West End, and that's the truth. . . ."

* * *

Outside the dock gates three brown men were explaining to the police in some unknown language that they desired to sleep in a ship that night, and through the gloom of the West India Dock Road drifted those furtive, suspicious figures with hunched shoulders and yellow faces and a walk that is almost a shuffle. . . .

Opium?

Or fried fish?

I must find out one of these nights.

Under Waterloo Bridge

LEAVE Piccadilly, its epileptic lights, its feverish, lost air of searching for something that it will never find, and go down to the Embankment on a clear night of stars. In the cold purity of this stillness the spirit is lifted and soothed. It is good to be alone in the night; it is good to feel sharp wind on the face; it is good to see the Plough flinging its clear symbol over a powdered sky . . . the dark bridges spanning the river; the only silver ripples from the moon; the oily golden ripples from the bridge lamps that shake and waver like swords beneath the waters.

The Thames at night is the most mysterious thing in London. So much part of London, yet so remote from London, so cold, so indifferent, so wise; for there is nothing about London that the Thames does not know. . . .

'Yes,' said the young police-sergeant, 'Waterloo Bridge has always had a kind of fascination. I suppose because the stone seats make it so easy to jump from. Many a time we've sat here watching people trying to make up their minds to jump, but, of course, we didn't know this till we'd fished them out and they had confessed that they'd been sitting there hour after hour trying to work up enough pluck.'

Against the windows of the little police pier known as Suicide Station, there was a steady, dark movement: the movement of the Thames going out to sea. Through the final span of Waterloo Bridge we saw, framed in that jet-black arch, a marvellous pastel of deep blues and blacks: the near lights of Hungerford Bridge, the more distant lamps of Westminster, the slow glide of a lit tramcar in the emptiness of the early morning.

I know of few more dramatic places in London at night than the Suicide Room of this police raft: the bed ready, the bath ready, the cordials ready, the little dinghy with the rubber roller at the stern, its nose pointed to the dark arches.

'Of course, since the bridge has been under repair things have been quiet, and in any case there are not half so many attempted suicides in the river as there used to be.'

I looked out at the steady, dark movement of the waters . . . sinister, indifferent Thames.

* * *

'A cigarette?'

'I'll smoke it later. . . . Of course, some come to themselves as soon as they touch the water. In fact, they mostly do—I suppose dying isn't nice once you start doing it! On the other hand, now and again they don't. It's generally the women that don't want to be saved; for when a woman makes up her mind to do a thing . . . I remember one night in summer . . .'

The chug-chug of the patrol boat sounded and ceased outside. We looked through the window and saw it and its shrouded crew of three rising and falling on the ebb tide.

'I remember one night in summer we heard a splash, and we were out in a second. She was a good-looking, nice-spoken young girl, but she *did* want to die. I've never seen anybody that wanted to die so much. She fought us and told us to go away; what right had we got to come interfering with her private affairs?—and all that sort of thing. She struggled so that it was a job to get the stern of the dinghy round to her. Have you ever tried saving anybody in a small boat? No; well, unless you grab 'em right you swamp the boat. Anyhow, we got her in, and she gave us a piece of her mind, sitting up with her hair all down and looking lovely—a treat she was. . . ."

He paused and looked earnest.

'When we got back,' he said, 'it was three o'clock in the morning.'

He stopped as if expecting comment.

'Well, why not?'

He leant forward earnestly, and I could tell that something serious was coming:

'Well, you see, the lady from Bow Street who undresses female suicides was off duty.'

'But the poor girl was half dead. Surely in a case like that . . .'

'No; she wasn't half dead! Only shock. I told you it was summer. You can't be too careful, you know. How did we know that she wouldn't get nasty for having her life saved, and complain that she had been treated disrespectfully?'

I tried hard not to smile. I could see his problem. I could also see his earnest, solemn face, anxious that I should see that problem.

'In addition to which,' he continued, 'all us fellows on duty that night were unmarried!'

Harder than ever, I tried not to smile! I was conscious that this was the best police story I had ever heard. I was torn between admiration for such fine feeling in a force often accused of callousness, and amusement at thought of the problem which confronted three young bachelors on a London morning.

'What did you do?' I asked.

'Well, we had a kind of consultation. She fainted. Something had got to be done at once, and none of us wanted to take the responsibility! Then we remembered Old Sam, who does odd jobs about the station. We went outside and found him. "Sam," we said, "you've been married, haven't you?" "Yes," he said. "Why?" "This is why," we said: "There's a young woman got to be undressed in the station, and it's you who've got to do it." "All right," said Old Sam, "I will."'

'And did he?'

'He did.'

'Is that the end of the story?'

'Yes.'

'Did the girl complain?'

'No, she didn't.'

'Why did she jump in?'

'I think,' said the young sergeant, tapping the cigarette on the desk, 'it was love. It mostly is with women.'

And he nodded towards the bridge that casts a varying shadow over Suicide Station.

* * *

Under Waterloo Bridge

I glanced back from the Embankment and saw the Thames heavy with the secrets it has carried to sea these thousand years, but so cold, so indifferent; and in the sky was a remote half-moon lying on its curve in a ridiculous and careless attitude, as if London did not mean anything.

A Jungle Night

YOU think that you know the Zoo. You have laughed at the bear who paws a bun through the bars ; you have watched the whiskered sergeant-major faces of the seals as they bark for fish ; you have seen the sleepy cats in the lion house, and you have, of course, noted the contempt in the tiger's amber eyes for you and all mankind.

Now I will show you the real Zoo ; I will show you a Zoo that no one in London knows or suspects ; I will show you a Zoo that lies in Regent's Park like a patch of primeval jungle older than Adam—the Zoo by the light of a full moon. . . .

The keeper unlocked a small wicket gate, and we went in. A white terrier called Bess, who adores a night rat hunt more than anything in the world, ran ahead and became lost to sight. The moon, clear of clouds, rode high above the spectral, black trees. A green wash of light fell over all things, casting shadows so black that a child might have tried to pick them up and carry them away ; cold, green winter moonlight.

It was at first quiet. The only sound was the tap of the keeper's stick on the path.

* * *

'What is that ?'

'A lion !' said the keeper.

A Jungle Night

The call came in the night so differently from the daytime howl for meat ; a wild, hot huskiness of two notes. It was an uncanny, savage hoarseness that vibrated in the night. It was difficult to locate : now it seemed to the left, now to the right. It was the kind of cry that would inevitably have drawn you into that lion's jaws had you been trying to escape from them ! There was a shuddering attraction about it, too. . . .

'Listen—she's answering him !' said the keeper. 'He's calling to a lioness !'

Through the night came a softer, shorter cry. We crept up quietly and saw them. He was sitting in the moonlight on a high rock—the magnificent, perfect savage—his great head in the air ; she was crouched against the bars in the next pen, very slim and slinky, watching him, then looking away, taking a walk and slinking back again to sit and admire him against the yellow moon.

She answered him from time to time through the bars—poor Thisbe !

'What do you think they are saying ?' I asked the keeper.

'I don't know,' he said.

But I do ! It was this :

'My dear,' he was saying, 'I would like to make love to you with newly killed meat, for the moon is full, and this is the time the deer go down to the salt licks. My paws are full of moonlight. They itch to tear something—for you, of course. How long is it since you tasted warm meat ?'

'Don't talk about it, dearest ! I feel like

killing, too! I would like to feel my body crouched against something not quite dead . . . you know that feeling, that rich, purring feeling. B-r-r-r-o-o-o-f-f-f!'

A savage love song under a little cold moon in Regent's Park.

* * *

A cloud scurried over and the light faded. There was a soft, furtive movement in the dark. Three feet away, close to the bars, crouched two leopards, their bodies pressed against the earth, their tails moving slowly from side to side like yellow snakes. I saw their unwinking eyes fixed on something beyond me, on Bess, the white terrier. Whenever she moved they moved with horrible intensity; the desire to kill in their noiseless scrutiny; every nerve in their bodies gathered in this desire.

In the next pen a tiger was crouched to spring; in the next a leopard lay full length on a rock and gazed up at the moon, his green eyes alight. The moon had brought the jungle into Regent's Park, and over these cages brooded the ancient instinct to stalk and kill, to tear and rend and fight. Such dear, sleepy cats by day, by night such murderers! I stood lost in a delicious horror. London was ten thousand years away.

Regent's Park was a little patch of country from the very dawn of time. It had nothing to do with London; it belonged to the heathen moon. In the air was the old law of tooth and claw. It was not horrible; it was vaguely exciting.

I was surprised to find myself thrilled as if the moon that had whispered the call of the wild to these beasts of prey had also touched some ancient memory in me ; something that could fear these creatures and yet admire and, in a way, respect them.

'Am I,' I asked myself, 'at the very secret of existence—this machine-like lust to exterminate—whence comes the brain and muscle to survive ? '

The great cats lay in wait . . . unblinking eyes watched our every movement; tails hit the earth.

We came to a bare tree shaking in the night wind. It was covered with dark objects like rooks' nests.

'Funny,' said the keeper, 'how the racoons refuse to sleep in the warm house we made for them, and climb that tree every night.'

I looked up and saw these little people, their tails twisted round the bare tree branches, their noses warm in their fur, fast asleep in the air, rocking this way and that across the moon. The instinct of their tribe! The whole of Regent's Park seemed to be given up to race memory . . . the call of the wild.

Even as I thought it there rose on the air the most blood-curdling cry that ever came from the throat of man or beast. It went up into the night like the essence of all ache and agony—a banshee wail. And it seemed to me that all the creatures became silent to listen, for it went on alone in the night, horrible, frightening.

'The big grey wolf!' whispered the keeper.

'He's going to howl for the moon. If we stand still we shall see and hear something in a minute!'

We stood in the shadow of a tree and saw him fling back on his haunches, lift his shaggy throat, and pour into the night all that was in his wild heart. . . . 'Ooooh,' he howled, 'Ooooooh to be running in green moonlight to-night, hungry in the snow, with the feel of the pack at my heels. . . .'

His cry was inexpressibly terrible, that long-drawn moan known in Scotland as the 'death howl'—a cry that dogs make when something old and sweetly miserable stirs in them and they forget the fireside and the bone buried in the garden. It wavered on the night air, beginning as a whine, rising to crescendo, and falling through every variation of ache and agony into a sudden bitten-off silence.

'Now you wait!' whispered the keeper. 'That will set them all off. Don't move. . . .'

The old grey wolf lifted his head again and opened his lean jaws, and this time he sang on and on, picking up his howl as it fell, and casting it back to the moon. And the song he sang was the song of a running scent and the swift, savage joy of a pack in full cry. . . . There were pine forests and moonlight in his song, soft snow drifted against the trees and ice on rivers in a lonely lost world far from Regent's Park! It was a call! The note of exile in it almost brought tears to the eyes; the savagery in it made a cold mane stand up on the spine. He called and he called with his gaunt muzzle lifted.

Then . . .

There were furtive, silent movements in the cages, little soft springings to earth and in each patch of moonlight in each cage sat a wolf.

The old wolf gave them the note, and they lifted up their voices in the old song. When he ceased they went on and on. The little white foxes sat up and yapped; the lumbering hyenas came into the moonlight and joined the chorus; the jackals whined and barked.

'We remember,' they seemed to howl in chorus. 'We remember what it is to run free in the light of the moon. . . .'

'Yap-yap!' yelped the little white foxes, pushing their black noses through the bars. . . . 'Yip-yip!' sang the small brown jackals; and the wolves, without ceasing, bayed the yellow moon. . . . My mind went far from London. I remembered standing one night of the full moon beside the Nile listening to the jackals in the Valley of the Dead challenging the dogs of Luxor from the opposite bank of the river. The dogs went wild with rage, and the little jackals sat out on the sand in the moonlight and barked back at them. All night long it went on till the mad moon faded.

* * *

'What do you think of it?' asked the keeper.

'Marvellous!' I whispered.

I wish the British Broadcasting Company would give this blood-curdling chorus to London on the night of the full moon. How it would chill the blood of Golders Green! I would also like to have a dog's opinion on it. It would be interesting to see how he would behave if he were awakened from the warmth of a fire to be introduced to his ancestors by a headphone. . . .

We walked towards them. The chorus stopped at once. Lean grey bodies leapt back into the shadows. All except one. 'Don't touch this animal' was written on his cage.

He dropped his voice and looked ashamed. (I did not know that a wolf could look sheepish!) He rubbed his rough sides against the bars and made the crying noise that collie dogs make when they want you to rub behind their ears.

'Old fellow!'

He whined in delight. I scratched his back and he danced with joy. I rubbed his nose for him and he said, 'Thank you,' just as any dog would say it.

'To-night he feels like being petted,' said the keeper, 'but to-morrow night he might feel like taking off your hand.'

Perhaps the moon had gone to his head.

* * *

We went on and came to a great island lifted above a deep pit. In the centre of the island were rocks and caves. The moonlight fell over it, making a miniature world of it.

A Jungle Night

'Seventy Madras baboons live there, but they are asleep,' said the keeper.

But he was wrong. A queer little old man's face peeped round the rock at us, and a queer little old man hunched out of the cave and came limping along with his big arms. He sat down on the edge of the island, hugged his stomach, looked up at the moon, scratched himself, and said something in a loud, harsh voice.

At the sound of his voice the whole tribe appeared in the mouth of the cave, incredibly weird and manlike. They peered with their whiskered faces and they stood bunched together in the narrow opening.

'Come on—it's only men!' the old baboon seemed to say to them.

They advanced in great disorder, rather timidly and slowly, and it seemed to me as I watched them in that pale light, fascinated by their uncanny little human faces, that I was seeing something that had happened long ago, before the first bludgeon had been discovered.

The little old man gave a curt nod to the moon, chattered something at us that sounded like an oath, and walked back over the moonlit rocks. The tribe retreated before him. The glimpse of history was over. . . .

* * *

Wild in the air sounded the song of the wolves in chorus above the homely trees of Regent's Park. The little gold moon looked down, and the green light that brings the jungle to London once a month lay over stick and stone—an even, green magic.

At a Stage Door

'TWENTY-FIVE years ago,' said the stage door-keeper, 'you had to be a regular pugilist on this job, and you needed a couple of first-class chuckers-out to help you through the evening. You just take a look out now, sir, and tell me what you see. . . .'

It was eleven-thirty. I pushed against the bar of the stage door and looked on a dark alleyway between a high wall and the entrance to the gallery. There was no one there! That is the story of the modern stage door: *there is no one there!*

'Twenty-five years ago,' continued the stage door-keeper, 'you could have looked through this window and seen at the end of the passage a row of hansom cabs waiting, and round the door here would be standing what we used to call the stage-door johnnies dressed in evening clothes, some of them in long black cloaks, and all of them holding bunches of flowers and black canes with silver tops. . . .'

'Our fathers,' I said reverently.

I suppose he would have confirmed this had he not been called to the telephone.

'Now it's *their* fathers,' he remarked, returning to the conversation.

'Whose fathers?' I asked.

'Why, the fathers of the chorus girls, of course. If it isn't a father it's an aunt. They call and take them home.'

'Times change,' I said.

'They do,' he agreed. 'You wouldn't hardly believe the number of golden quids I've taken through that door just to run up with a note. There was one little fellow whom the girls used to call the "Rat", but his real name was Lord Whortleberry. He had a lisp, and he was awful sweet on Harriet N——, and he used to hate waiting, but was frightened that one of the other johnnies would go off with her. "Tell Hawiet to huwy," he used to say, and she used to say when I told her, "Tell the Wat to go to hell." And one day I did tell him, and he went off with Harriet's chum, a lovely girl of the name of Gubbins. There was a fair old shindy, and in less than a week Harriet had married him. "If it hadn't been for you, John," she said once when she called here in her carriage, "I'd never have left the chorus, and I don't know whether I ought to give you a fiver or a thick ear." I winked at her and said, "Well, my lady, if you takes my advice . . ."'

'Trrrrrrng!' went the telephone.

The promoter of dynasties answered it.

* * *

The door behind the keeper's box opened, releasing that lively scent of peardrops that fills all theatres. Two plain maidens stood waiting. The stage door opened and a meek little middle-aged face with a wispy, mouse-coloured moustache appeared:

'Come along, girls,' said the face.

'All right, Dad,' said the girls.

They went.

'That's how it is now,' said the stage door-keeper. 'Mind, I'm not saying it isn't better, but—it's not so exciting!'

A young man's head appeared out of the night:

'Miss Robinson ready yet, John?'

'Not yet.'

The head shot back into the outer darkness.

'Now that's the nearest thing to a stage-door johnny we've got to-day,' explained John. 'He's the fellow Miss R.'s engaged to. He sits in the pit three nights a week—or the gallery if he's broke—and waits to take her home.'

The door leading to the cold stone steps that mount to the dressing-rooms was flung open and out came a lovely long-legged vision in an inadequate kimono. She put twopence down on the janitor's desk and taking up the telephone demanded Brixton.

'Is that you, Mum? What's for supper? Tripe? Can you get any beer? I'm bringing Mr. de Courcey Potts home for supper. Don't let Dad see him if he's a bit—you know? S'long.'

The vision faded upwards in flying kimono.

* * *

Through the door burst a number of pretty young girls chattering of last trams and trains.

They disappeared down the empty alleyway.

Then came from the dressing-rooms a pale masculine flapper of about twenty-five. He took up the telephone and spoke with the voice of the spurious Etonian :

'Hallo, old dear. Courcey Potts speaking. I can't come along to-night ; I'm going on to supper somewhere. So long, old darling ! '

'You wouldn't think he was a chorus " gent ", would you ? ' said the door-keeper.

* * *

Round the stage door rose the sound of feminine chatter.

'The gallery girls,' said John.

Gallery girls. They have replaced the johnny ! They pursue their favourites with schoolgirl heroine worship ! Down came the 'star'. She plunged into their adoration and disappeared among them in the direction of a taxicab.

One by one the lights went out.

The stage door stood with an experienced air, as if conscious of the glamour it had cast over the Victorian Age ; as if aware that in the stately homes of Old England . . .

'Good night, sir,' cried the stage door-keeper, his boots ringing on the empty flagstones.

Night in Hospital

WHEN you pass a London hospital at night think of this. . . .

The wards are darkened. The nurse goes tiptoe over the polished floor between the two white shrouded ranks. It is very quiet. Now and again she passes a bed, congratulating life in general that the occupant is sleeping, only to find two wide-awake eyes fixed on her in the dimness : eyes that follow her hungrily anxious that she shall not go and leave no focus for thought ; eyes which plead not to be abandoned to the horror of a darkness in which the sore mind reels and plunges like a ship at sea.

Night turns sleepless people into poor frightened children. The nightmare of the sleepless is a much more terrifying thing than the nightmare of the dreamer ; for awake we make our own grotesque hell consciously, and there is reason in it.

Of all the agonies suffered by London in the night I would place first those waking nightmares of the hospital ward when a man or a woman lost to companionship waits miserably for the first grey streak of dawn.

'Sister, speak to me, say *something* to me. . . .'

Is there a more pathetic cry in the night of London ?

There come moments in all lives when we can touch beauty and godliness—unconsciously, perhaps, and as a matter of course—and this moment in the life of a hospital nurse comes in the darkened ward when her cool woman's hand stretched out over the white sheet has the power to lead a soul out of a tortured Gethsemane into the mercy of sleep.

* * *

Grotesque humour and deep heartache follow each other through the wards at night. . . .

It is that 'nerve' period between eleven p.m. and four a.m., the time when human vitality is at its lowest, when the tide of life so often ebbs. And the nurse sits there watching over every kind of possibility.

The large man with d.t.'s has just called her up and asked her to remove the snake from the bunch of bananas that grows over the foot of his bed; the delirious patient has just stripped off his clothes and expressed a desire to run down to Brighton for a bathe; and in many a bed there are sighs; and sleepers turn restlessly as though that Angel of the Small Hours is passing down the ward with a faint rustle of wings.

Now drama! In the next ward the nurse goes to a bed. The signs for which she has been ordered to watch are there! She must act at once! In a second she is speaking to the doctor on duty. He comes quickly to bend over the bed. Here and there heads on pillows turn to watch as the sleepless ones dimly sense this battle in the night going on about them: this splendid fight waged night after night in hospitals when skill and science mobilize against death. Yes; it is touch and go. An immediate operation is necessary! Relatives must be warned! The police in the district in which they live are instructed to awaken them.

In Harley Street a famous surgeon picks up the receiver by his bedside, and into a brain dull with sleep is borne the swift knowledge that he must go out at once to fight with his mind and with his deft fingers. Being a man he may say 'Damn', but, being a doctor, he never says 'No'; and over him, as he hurries into clothes and into the waiting motor-car, is something more splendid than you will find in London all night through. Harley Street may bleed the rich, but the specialist often gives his knowledge to the poor.

A clock strikes three! London is asleep! In the brilliant light of the operating theatre the surgeon, sharply awake in every nerve, picks up an instrument and bends over the body of a young girl whose life seems gathered in the points of his fingers. The actors in this splendid drama, hurriedly assembled from sleep, stand shrouded in white garments. . . . Silently, efficiently, they go about the white room; and there is no sound but the sharp tinkle of metal on glass and the noise of liquids boiling. . . .

The clock strikes the half-hour.

'Yes, she will live,' they tell the relatives. 'She will live.'

* * *

Down in the casualty ward is comedy.

Casualties arrive in three waves at night in a centrally situated London hospital: the before eleven o'clock casualties, which represent the final kicks delivered by London before bedtime on her careless or unfortunate children; the after eleven o'clocks, mainly due to strong drink and staircases; and the after three a.m. casualties from Covent Garden and night workshops, which represent the first kicks delivered by London at the opening of a new day.

I say there is comedy. There is the comedy of the policeman who thinks he has brought in an epileptic, and discovers that his patient is just a plain, ordinary drunk; there is the tragi-comedy of the old crook, who summons up more symptoms than any hypochondriac in order to occupy one of the few casualty ward beds for a night:

'Then I comes all over dizzy and I can't stand, and the pain at me 'eart is just like a knife twisted.'

How many young doctors new to night casualty work have cheated a deserving case out of a bed by giving the old Embankment hand the benefit of the doubt? And the news of a soft-hearted hospital doctor flies round homeless circles like an arrow from the bow.

* * *

Then . . .

'Make way there. . . . Tip up your end, Bill. . . . Mind that doorpost!'

On the stretcher is a girl, deathlike, on whose face rouge and powder are grotesque. The forms of the policemen who have brought her through the London night bulk largely in the narrow passage. The young doctor and the nurses are bending over something red wrapped round her throat.

'Yes, we got him,' say the police. 'He didn't know what he'd done. He cried like a kid. . . . Bow Street. Has he killed her?'

The door opens. A nurse comes out white-faced, wide-eyed. The door closes. The drama goes on. . . .

In a few hours dawn comes up over London in a wave of pearl-pale light.

Fan-tan

I DINED in a smart West End hotel, exchanged a silk hat for a cap in the cloak-room, and in half an hour was enjoying one of London's strangest contrasts—Limehouse.

As I walked on through dark streets it seemed impossible that the grill-room I had left, with its elegant women, its discreet string orchestra, its air of assured comfort and well-being, could exist in the same world with these gloomy avenues, like a slum in hell, through which shivering lascars shuffled, hugging the shadows, while Chinamen with their mask faces and their sharp eyes peered from dim doorways into the night. . . .

I am not attempting to add to the romance of Limehouse, because there is no romance there; only squalor and the pathos of poor, frightened odds and ends of humanity whose lives are spent in the bowels of ships, whose pleasures consist in being stranded for three days in London, Yokohama, or Jamaica while their ships unload. It cannot matter to them where they are, for all their gambling dens are the same, and they go from ship to den and from den to ship. They are modern galley slaves, and their eyes are either sharp and shifty or sad and brown like the eyes of monkeys.

Before the war Limehouse had a Chinese population of twenty-five hundred. To-day its population is two hundred and fifty. An Order in

Council of 1916 made it an offence to smoke opium. Since then Limehouse has gone to pieces.

* * *

The squalor of Limehouse is that strange squalor of the East which seems to conceal vicious splendour. There is an air of something unrevealed in those narrow streets of shuttered houses, each one of which appears to be hugging its own dreadful little secret. As you go on through them, past hunched figures who give way before you, it seems that at any moment you might stumble on the key to the mystery ; that you might open a filthy door and find yourself in a dim palace sweet with joss-sticks, where queer things happen in a blue mist of smoke.

On the other hand, you would not be surprised to know that such things have never been, for Limehouse—that dirty tentacle which the East has flung into London—exerts that spell of provocative mystery which is the gift of the ancient East to the youthful imagination of the West.

* * *

In the doorway leaned a gigantic negro who had smoked his cigar to the band. He rolled his eyes at me and moved aside. He lifted a hand to his cigar : there were only three fingers on it ! I drew aside a curtain of old sacking and found myself in a narrow hall, bare as the hall of an empty house. On the banister was a card bearing two Chinese hieroglyphs stating that the game of fan-tan was in progress.

Every other house in Pennyfields bears this sign at night. This short street which links the West India Dock Road with Poplar High Street is the Monte Carlo of East London.

In the gaming-room—a mean, shuttered apartment at the back of the house—twenty coloured men were bending over a table in front of a blazing fire, watching the board with an intensity which linked them with the International Sporting Club. The banker, a little Chinaman whose face looked like a handbook on smallpox, had that far-off expression which you will see on the face of all croupiers, as if in close communion with the gods of chance. His eyes took in every face in a flash. He saw me and his eyes flickered in surprise, but he never ceased play!

The gamblers put shillings on the numbers one, two, three, or four. The banker took a fistful of small buttons and counted them in fours. The uneven number remaining after he had counted his last set of four determined the winners, and he paid those men who had put money on this number. Long before he had reached his count, when yet there remained under his hand a confused pile of buttons, the keen eyes of the fan-tan fans had sorted them, spotted the result, and their hands were ready for the money!

I wondered what would happen if the bank went broke; and I judged the distance to the door!

* * *

Half the players were Chinamen, but not the Chinamen of romance. They wore soft hats and collars and ties. Some of the teeth present suggested to me that opium is still smoked. There were four or five stumpy brown West Indian niggers and one coal-black coon with the thickest lips I have ever seen. They looked like two grey pneumatic tyres.

He was a champion player. I saw him win sixteen shillings in ten minutes.

'You're a lucky player,' I said to him.

'I guess ah'm a good speculator, suh!' he replied with a perfect Charleston accent.

'Where do you come from?' I asked.

That was my one mistake. The gambling den's attitude towards me changed in the most swift and subtle fashion. They were willing to tolerate my presence, but not my questions. I quite agreed with them!

'Come over in the teak ship, suh!' he said resentfully.

Two Chinamen slipped out.

Dozens of mild, brown, monkey eyes were fixed on me. I smiled. They smiled. They nodded their heads and the smiles broadened. In their smiling politeness I read the thought: 'We do wish you would go away, because we don't know who you are and we don't particularly like you.'

I took the hint.

The big nigger at the door asked for a match to revive the last half-inch of his cigar, and he took one with his horrible hand.

* * *

I went into six other dens in the space of twenty yards. They were all the same: a front room in which melancholy lascars and Chinamen were painting out the hieroglyphs on pucka-pu cards; a back room in which they were crouched over the swifter results of fan-tan.

Such silence in den and in street; the uncanny silence of people who do not think as we think, whose ways are not our ways. The silence grips you, almost persuading you that behind it is something which you are always on the verge of discovering; some mystery of vice or of beauty, or of terror and cruelty; something more than those mild, monkey eyes bent on piles of shillings. . . .

The red omnibus at the corner of the West India Dock Road took me back to London for threepence, and I came home with the belief that if all the things written about Limehouse are not true, they ought to be!

Drama on Wheels

PICCADILLY is empty. That throbbing pulse of London life is stilled ; a lingering, painted woman stands on the cold corner of Regent Street, and two policemen walk slowly towards Leicester Square. . . .

It is the time when the taxicab cruising softly by the kerb from the darkness of the Green Park becomes the most dramatic thing in London. The omnibuses have stopped ; there are no tubes. Through the dark, unnatural streets quests the taxicab, linking lover to lover, crook to crook, criminal to criminal. It is a drama on wheels. At any moment a figure may materialize from the deadness that is London, and a lifted finger or a raised cane will call the taxicab to swifter motion, turn its bonnet towards Houndsditch or Park Lane.

The man at the wheel sits like a blind knight-errant of the streets at the service of good or evil. . . .

He does not know the whys and wherefores of his small-hour pilgrimages—the surprising places he may be asked to visit do not excite his imagination, for it is all in the night's work ! He rescues a damsel in cold distress and takes her to Curzon Street, he picks up an unsteady man and takes him home to a furious wife in Hampstead ; he meets a suspicious couple and deposits them in a snug little suburban villa ; he carries a cheery, honest, hail-fellow-well-met character to the grimness of a deserted mansion. . . .

He picks up the odds and ends of London and tidies up the empty streets ; only now and then, when a King's Counsel rises in court and says : 'Gentlemen of the jury, you will hear the evidence of the taxicab driver who was chartered by the prisoner in Piccadilly at two a.m. on the night in question '—only then does the taxicab driver emerge as the genius of the London night whose hands steer tragedy through dead streets.

Blind knight of London. . . .

* * *

It was warm and cosy in the cab-shelter. Now and again the moon of some passing headlight would wax and wane through the frosted glass of the windows. The place smelt of sausage and mash, gunpowder coffee, damp overcoats and sawdust. It was blue with smoke, and as fuggy as a French bedroom.

The taxicab drivers sat in their coats, their caps pushed back on their heads. They ate sausages (and anything else that was ready), and they drank coffee from thick cups.

The London taxicab man is a fine fellow. He suffered badly during the war from the reputation of a bad type of driver who had the instincts of Dick Turpin ; but with demobilization that kind of man was weeded out of the business, and to-day the taxicab man is a credit to London. He is an interesting fellow to talk to, for he holds so many secrets of London. There is a rather fine conspiracy of silence in the profession: a driver never splits on a fare. Doctors and taxi-drivers never tell!

'Though it's surprising how some well-known people go about London not thinking that we recognize them . . . the places I've taken some people to who wouldn't like it in the papers—pass the matches, Bill!"

(You can have all the elegant conversation you like, but give me the queer, disjointed, half-expressed confabulations of policemen, taxicab men, bargees, and others who move about London at strange hours. . . .)

'Only once a fellow killed himself in my cab. . . . I picked him up outside one of the big clubs along Piccadilly late at night, and he seemed a bit queer. I thought that he'd been having a drop too much. He gave me an address in Bayswater, and when I got there he didn't get out, and I hadn't heard a sound. I thought he was asleep—I hadn't seen his face then—and when I shook him a revolver fell out of his coat.'

Nobody seemed interested. They sat round, chewing and swallowing.

'The funniest thing that ever happened to me in that line,' said a driver, 'was when I picked up a fare in the Haymarket one night, a lady she was by the look of her—but you can't tell one from the other these days, can you?—and when we got half-way where we were going she tapped on the window and I slowed up. "Driver," she said, "I wish you'd take care of this for me," and she handed out a little pistol no bigger than my pipe.'

He took a great gulp of coffee.

'What did I do? Well, I didn't know what to do! What would you have done? I didn't want to tell a cop because there's no knowing what mightn't have happened, so I just went on and when she got out she asked me for the pistol. "Look here, miss," I said, "you let me throw this 'ere away or you may get into a mess." She went up in a fine rage. "Don't be insolent," she said. "Do you suppose I want to shoot myself? It isn't loaded, but I've borrowed it in case burglars break in as I'm living all alone—and I don't like the feel of it!"'

* * *

Then they began describing in broken sentences the strange places to which they had been ordered at night—places they had not known of before, places that suggested even to their matter-of-fact minds that 'something was going on. . . .'

'That was a funny job I had the other night I was telling Jim about. A bloke in a silk hat comes running up to me in Regent Street at about one-thirty and tells me to go to an address in Hampstead as quick as lightning. When we get there we turn up a long, dark drive and come to a big house with all the windows barred—one of those barracky places that they are turning into flats. There wasn't a blinking sound. The fare hammered on the door and nothing happened. I got down and gave him a hand, but the place seemed to be empty. Then we heard a dog bark —one of those little lap-dogs by the yap of it— and then another one; a deep bark that I knew was a big dog. The fellow got very excited, and started running down the steps and looking up at the windows, but there was no light. And the dogs went on playing hell. . . .

'Then they stopped and a window in a shrubbery lit up. We ran down a side path. The window was a kitchen window; it had bars down it, and on the other side of it was a girl who had just got out of bed. She had put a pink silk thing over her nightdress, and under one arm was a Pekinese barkin' fit to bust, and standing beside her looking through the window was the biggest bloodhound you ever saw. My fare went up to the window, which she opened, and said something to her. I tried to hear what it was but couldn't, but she seemed to be giving him a proper old telling-off. . . . He got back into the cab and I dropped him at Regent Street, where I found him! Now what do you make of that? I call that funny I do!'

* * *

Through the silent streets of London they go . . . at any moment Comedy, Tragedy, Mystery may come to the kerbstone and lift a finger to them.

Cabaret

WE must not miss a fashionable London cabaret.

It is ten p.m., which used to be considered fairly late. The place is empty because it is too early. Three or four couples move timidly in each other's arms over the small dance floor under the critical Italian eyes of an army of relaxed waiters. Nothing happens till midnight; but Sutton, Kensington, Manchester, and Liverpool have contrived to form a thin crust of humanity at the inner circle of tables. Beyond this circle hundreds of little gold chairs wait to be sat on; hundreds of white tables stand ready for oysters and plover; hundreds of glasses are waiting for their champagne.

We admire the 'niceness' of the English girl and the pinkness of the young man who is in love with her, and we wonder how life will go with them and how dull they will be in time. A middle-aged man, who should deny his tailor nothing, glides round with a young girl who possesses the eyes and mouth of a chartered accountant. We wonder if his wife cares.

Corpulent elderly people, who fifty years ago would have been at least resigned, hug each other like bears and bob defiantly in the direction of their old age. The band whines and whinnies and underneath it is the steady rhythm of Africa. We chase away the feeling that we are watching something happening long ago in a forest clearing as we gaze round for somebody to dance with; because nothing is quite so funny as the act of dancing till you become involved in it. . . .

* * *

It is now nearly midnight.

In one hour and a half the atmosphere of the room has changed. It is now packed with people. All the little gold chairs and the little white tables are occupied by the after-theatre crowd. Social self-consciousness has been replaced by social curiosity. The slightly-warm front row turns and regards the quite-cool back rows with furtive interest. Here and there above the olives and the Martinis and the lobster mayonnaise are well-known faces; faces which most mornings gaze upon the British Isles from the newspapers.

Look at Lady X! Age is the last thing that matters about her; she has that marvellous American poise; she makes all the 'nice' girls of twenty-five look pale. The girl in shell pink who appeared quite interesting at ten o'clock is now toneless as we watch Lady X leaning, her fine lips slightly parted, her experienced eyes narrowed as she inhales cigarette smoke nervously and quickly dabs the cigarette to death with a flicker of diamonds on white fingers. . . .

The band throbs, the audacious saxophone blows out little velvet-lined sentimentalities which are surely in league with French vineyards. The lights go down. The small floor becomes a mass of moving people. There is a clatter of plates, a popping of corks, a great hum of talk; and the waiters go swiftly over the thick carpet, bearing food which at this time of night would have killed the Victorians stone dead.

We of this syncopated period may have poor souls, but our digestions are ahead of history.

* * *

Midnight!

The band stops and the lights go down; the cabaret is due. A London night is about to close on an adequate vision of lovely women.

'It costs us fifty pounds a week in silk stockings,' whispers the producer in the darkness. 'Can't allow one ladder in this show.'

The curtains at the end of the room part, there is an encouraging burst of melody from the band, and out glide a crowd of genuinely lovely girls dressed in musical comedy pyjamas. They look like a box of selected peaches in a Bond Street fruit shop.

'Well, I've seen a few shows on Broadway,' whispers an American, 'but this bunch beats the band!'

They sing. They dance. They go. The dim crowd of white shirt fronts and the faint blur of white arms move restlessly in applause. A delicious girl comes out and dances round the room, her short skirt brushing the inner ring of tables. Turn follows turn. It is a thumbnail revue. It is clever, it is pretty, but it would not matter much if it were neither with a chorus like a box of picked peaches. It is strange how the idea of feminine beauty changes age by age ; it would be amusing for the producer to contrast his essentially modern, shingled, lamp-post chorus with a chorus of the kind that drove our fathers to the stage door thirty years ago.

The peaches mass for the finale. They crowd towards the tables and point fingers round at the white shirt fronts and the white shoulders, singing : 'Keep it up . . . keep it up. . . .'

The revellers applaud discreetly and with great decorum ; as long as it is perfectly good form to keep it up they will carry on ! This is not Parisian : it is merely an acquired habit : something that grew up out of London's post-War restlessness ; out of London's passionate determination to resist the temptation of going home. The lights flood the room, the dance band gathers itself and leaps into fractured excitement ; the floor fills. . . .

* * *

Outside it is very cold, an old man is selling matches, the Thames is dark under a clouded half-moon, and the night becomes a reality.

The First Edition ◇ ◇ ◇ ◇

IT is that time of night when the wives of newspaper men—that noble army of martyrs—have placed Daddy's slippers before a stoked-up fire and have retired to dream that they had been sensible and had married the rich brass-founder with no enthusiasm, who ceased work prompt at five—as all married men should do! Poor Fleet Street wives! It must be like marriage with a famous bigamist. How difficult when children ask: 'Who is that man who comes here to sleep?'

* * *

In Fleet Street it is zero hour: the first edition is just going over the top into a new day. The omnibuses have ceased running and the arc lights hanging overhead across the street illuminate an empty road bright with the lit windows of the world's 'London Offices'. Behind these windows men are pumping news into Adelaide, Winnipeg, Washington, New York, Berlin, Paris, Dublin, Liverpool, Cairo, and Hong-Kong.

In alleyways wait groups of cloth-capped men, who stand about furtively like hired assassins met on a dark occasion; drawn up to the kerb-stone are motor-lorries and vans. In a few minutes the newspapers, warm and damp and smelling most gloriously of ink, will come pouring from the great presses, folded and counted. Then will begin that nightly race to the mail trains, which spread the daily snow-storm of information and opinion over the length and breadth of the British Isles.

Fleet Street at this time is the only live street in the City of London; yet it looks so quiet, so different from the Fleet Street of fiction which is always 'shaking' like a wet retriever. No difficult operation is so quietly performed as the production of a newspaper. You might walk down Fleet Street at midnight and never guess the madness and frenzy behind it; in its most hectic hour it seems a street of secrets, a street hugging to its breast the 'beats' of to-morrow.

Only when you turn down an unpromising alley do you hear the treble scream of a metal cylinder as it meets the trimming knife; only then do you smell the important smell of a matrix turned silver: only then do you glimpse in a well-lit yard ranks of waiting lorries and a crowd of men standing before an ominous open door . . . beyond, in a mauve light of mercury vapour lamps, are big machines almost ready to tell to-day about yesterday.

* * *

In offices, centrally heated by the cigars of dramatic critics, calm young Scotsmen in horn-rimmed glasses, who since four p.m. have heard the whole world speaking at once and have rejected (or 'spiked') or accepted (or 'sent-up') its varied remarks, lean back and put down their pencils. In twenty minutes the great ship will be launched, and nothing on earth can catch the first edition—if St. Paul's fell down, if the House of Lords caught fire, if the franc went back to par, not a line. . . . Oh, ghastly thought. . . .

The tape machine and the post office pile up the agony; the mound of events grows higher; the sub-editors go through it listlessly as clerks handle cables when the liner is 'cast-off' from the dock side. Still, you never know. . . . Hell! A young man at the foreign desk casts a look of terror at the clock and dives out with a telegram in his hand!

'Yes?' asks the night editor, with the shattering coolness of a doctor at a childbirth.

'The Emir of Karaheesh has been shot by his favourite wife!' cries the young man.

'Really?' says the night editor. 'Rush page one.'

He touches a button. Another young man comes in.

'Oh, Robinson, when you were at the Foreign Office did you ever meet the Emir of Karaheesh?'

'I was with the British Mission to Karaheesh, sir.'

'Then write ten lines—no more, mind—for the second edition on the life and the habits of the Emir. I suppose you never met his chief wife?'

'No, sir.'

'Ah, what a pity. . . . Never mind!'

* * *

A fire engine runs up Holborn.

A vague street lounger smelling of remote beer stands panting in the waiting-room.

'British Musheum's on fire!' he says, holding out his hand for ten shillings. 'Heard it from a cop on Ludgate Hill.'

The night news editor looks at him sadly and goes to his telephone. He then calls a reporter.

'A boarding-house is on fire in Bloomsbury,' he says. 'You have fifteen minutes to get two lines in the Stop Press.'

(Who ever appreciates the gallant agonies of the young men—often delicately brought up and well educated—who fight by night to get two lines in the 'fudge'?)

* * *

Hark!

There they go! They start slowly, grindingly, accelerate in two seconds, and reach a deep, uniform roar—the machines! The first edition is flicking through their oily entrails; and the waiting men in the street outside crank up the lorries. It seems as if a sudden fresh breeze has invaded the newspaper office as the throbbing machines go pounding on; for this is the sound you never, never forget when you marry a newspaper—the voice of your first wife.

In the editorial room a group of men recalls Rembrandt's 'Lesson in Anatomy.' On the operating table lies the first edition. The editor in the centre of eager heads marks this and that, deletes here, amends there. A young newspaper is the only birth on which men immediately hold an inquest!

* * *

Then Fleet Street in the early hours, St. Paul's riding high above the City, and little lost winds pulling at street corners. . . .

Men go home through the Street, which Mr James Bone has so rightly called the 'village street'—the street of the village pump—and, as they go home, some, in this tired, sentimental hour, think of the dreams lost there and the dreams that almost came true.

Here it is that Dick Whittington would have come to-day to snatch the bright promise of glory, that seems to hang—quite invisibly—somewhere between the 'Griffin' and Ludgate Hill. . . .

A lorry changes gear and dashes on to Euston like a dispatch rider. Beneath the ground the great presses throb and pound . . . the voice of Fleet Street, the voice of Power, the astonishing thunder of the Press.

A Lost Day

IF you roam Piccadilly at night looking lonely and innocent you will meet various well-worn characters; young men who overdo a careful Oxford accent, and eventually suggest a game of cards; three men who are dying to 'let you in' on a good thing because they took a fancy to you right off ('only it needs capital, old boy'); twinkling, middle-aged men with an over-stressed man-about-town air who hint that when you 'know the ropes'—and they would not mind showing them to you this very night, being at a loose end for once—'when you know the ropes, old fellow, Paris isn't in it!'

Unclean people! They make you want an immediate cold bath!

There is the little vampire with the hard mouth and the big eyes and the cheap scent who slips an arm through yours and, finding you soft-hearted, tells you the story of a country vicarage—one of Piccadilly's oldest stories—and if you can forget Charles Garvice and believe that you are hearing these details for the first time she may swagger off with the Treasury note on which her poor heart is set.

There are, however, other chance acquaintances of a London night who have no mean motives. They just want to talk, and some day I would like to make a book of all the unsolicited stories I have heard from strangers in Piccadilly.

* * *

The young man wore the hat of a genius—an old felt horror, with a stained band and a limp crown, the battered survivor of a thousand riots and revels.

It was this hat that interested me as I sat opposite the young man in a Piccadilly café. It interested me because it could not have looked more out of place with the rest of him had it been a Life Guard's helmet. It was not the kind of hat this type of young man wears—it was the hat that goes with soiled shirt-cuffs and a soul. This young man was, with the exception of his alien hat, a prosperous, rather smug, business man from, I judged, Bradford.

He was drinking beer, and when he lifted the glass his hand trembled. Every now and then he looked at me, wishing to speak, but he thought better of it, and looked away quickly like a dog that has not made up his mind to wag his tail. He had a simple face, and he looked round the smoky café, its drinking, laughing crowd, with rather wide, surprised eyes. Two girls sitting at the next table had summed him up as 'soft' and were giggling. Then he spoke to me.

Yes, it was getting colder. Probably freezing. Colder in London than in the north. . . .

His accent was faintly provincial. He leaned forward:

'Would you, sir, have a drink with me?'

I said I would. We went on talking.

*   *   *

A Lost Day

The young man put down his glass.

'See how my hand trembles,' he said.

'I know,' I replied. 'Your nerves are bad.'

'As a matter of fact,' he said, in a low, matter-of-fact voice, 'I have been dead for twenty-four hours. I am terribly worried about it.'

I thought at first that he was probably mad, but his eyes reassured me.

'To-day's Wednesday,' he said. 'The last thing I can remember is Monday. I can just remember going to bed on Monday night, and I woke up this morning in my hotel at Paddington, and when I looked at the newspaper I saw it was Wednesday. What did I do yesterday? I think I may have been out and about, but—I don't remember a blessed thing! I was so dashed drunk on Monday night that my brain was a blank for a whole day!'

The mild young man laughed in a half-ashamed way.

'On Monday,' he went on, 'I came to London from —— to attend a wedding. I didn't know anybody there save the bride and bridegroom, and afterwards I went round London drinking. I put down an awful lot, and mixed them too. I then remember getting back to my hotel. That was Monday night. I awakened this morning feeling a bit dizzy; and it's Wednesday, isn't it? What I want to know is: where was I yesterday?'

'Perhaps you were in a kind of a trance,' I suggested.

'I thought of that. But when the chamber-maid brought me tea this morning she said nothing,

The hotel people said nothing. If I had been in a trance yesterday the hotel would have brought a doctor to me.'

'Why don't you ask them what happened?'

'I don't like to. I'm rather ashamed; and, besides, look at this!'

He picked up the battered felt hat.

'Well, what about it?'

'It isn't mine. I don't know whose it is. I found it on the bed-post this morning! Now it seems to me that, although my brain was dead all yesterday, I must have got up as usual, dressed, shaved, and gone out. Where? Goodness only knows! I have been wandering all over London to-day trying to think things out, hoping that my memory would come back; for it's awful not to know. And this hat! It's a terrible hat, isn't it? and I've been so worried that I have not bought a new one! I feel somehow that if I stick to the thing I may remember something of yesterday.'

'Has anything like this happened to you before?"

'Only in France, when I was knocked out.'

He looked at his watch.

'I've got to get over to Paddington,' he said. 'I'm going home. If ever you are in —— do look me up."

He gave me a business card. He got up, smiled in a puzzled way, and went out into Piccadilly Circus.

* * *

A Lost Day

As I went out into Piccadilly I thought how unpleasant it must be to feel that you were about London for a whole day with a dead brain covered by a strange ominous hat.

'Sir Percivale'

'SIR PERCIVALE' comes thundering up through Kent, the night Continental boat train behind him, his lean, lithe one hundred and twenty-nine tons flung out over the track like a running leopard; and he sings as he runs:

I'm bringing you home,
To England, to England,
I'm bringing you home,
To London, to London . . .
Bringing you home, bringing you home, bringing you home. . . .

The line of his lit Pullman cars is like a string of pearls flashed through the hop-fields, whipped through the night against the Pilgrims' Way; and he comes so regularly, and goes so swiftly, that only the newest born rabbits at the edge of woods dream of showing their little tails to him. He is not as heavy as the 'Caerphilly Castle' or as famous as the 'Flying Scotsman,' but to me he is a poem in steel, for in the roar of his wheels, if you know him well, is the most lovely song in all the world, a song of silver olive trees and white roads in Spain, the sun on ripe oranges, the camels humping in from deserts with the date harvest, snow on Lebanon, dawn on Carmel, the moon caught up in the palm trees on the beach at Haifa, and the little lost sadnesses played on flutes by boys beside the Nile. . . .

* * *

‘ Sir Percivale ’

He stands in Victoria covered with the sweat of his run, his six-foot-seven driving wheels moist with green oil, his great connecting and side rods silver with effort, his pistons bright, the flanges of his bogie wheels white as new shillings. . . .

(Women go to the Customs and declare the Paris *lingerie* in registered trunks, the crowds kiss and go, the last taxi disappears. . . .)

A squat little shunter departs with the Pullman cars ; and ‘ Sir Percivale ’, with a mighty snort and a puff of sudden steam, backs his long leanness out of Victoria into that place where all engines go at night to be fussed and washed and patted and bathed and made ready for new miles.

* * *

‘ Hi, Bill, here’s the Continental ! ’

In the smoky darkness of the vast Locomotive Beauty Parlour—one of the largest in the country—a grimy mechanic runs to the huge turn-table and places it in position as ‘ Sir Percivale ’ swings in over the points with a low escape of steam, that sounds like the whinny of a horse in sight of oats. He sinks on the turn-table with a noise like a house falling, and the great circle revolves with him as sweetly as a roulette wheel turns, leading him to a track that will take him to the repair sheds.

Far off the repair sheds expose roof lights in a steam of damped furnaces. There is a sound of released pressure and hammers.

‘ Sir Percivale ’ puffs slowly on, the men who

have brought up the boat train lean out of the high cab. Cleaners run up.

'The old gal's running a treat . . . puffing her head off!'

(I shudder to hear 'Sir Percivale' called 'old gal'!)

The fireman and the driver climb down, oil cans and leather bags in their hands. The driver walks to the great wheels and opens a little oil box and snaps the lid again. I watch his competent hand on the smooth flank of his giant.

'She's a fair treat!' he says to the old cleaner; 'you should have heard her humming up to Shepherd's Well. . . .'

They rake out the furnaces, they board the engine, they wash, they wipe and polish, as fussy as a bunch of ladies' maids.

On parallel tracks are other locomotives: 'King Arthurs', heavy goods, 'mixed traffic', humble suburbans, and little tanks. They take their places in the sheds in the order of their going forth again. All night long they arrive or leave; all night long the giant turn-table revolves in the darkness, bringing them home or sending them out on the road—to the south, to the west. . . .

* * *

'Here's the nine forty-five from Exeter!'

A shadow like a moving cathedral looms into the shed, bearing a yellow lamp.

'Make way there; tell Clapham I'm coming!' says a sharp escape of steam, and there is a grinding of wheels and a few heavy puffs.

‘Sir Percivale’

‘There goes the engine of the fish train. Picks up the Grimsby train at Clapham and takes her on in the night!’

Among the sleeping, sleek giants is here and there a roar of re-fired furnaces, in many a cab the stokers work in a red glow like shovelling devils, one eye on the coal stack and the other on the rising gauges. . . .

‘Good-bye, you lazy slackers!’ cries the engine of the Southampton night mail. ‘I’m off with the King’s mails! If you’ve any news for the next Cunarder look sharp about it!’

‘Pretentious ass,’ growls ‘Sir Percivale’, with his last inch of steam. ‘I take the mails to France, and if we’re late we’re “for it”. . . . Southampton? Where’s that? All down hill from Litchfield! How would he like to catch the boat over a switchback of one in a hundred . . . up and down to Dover? . . .’

‘And I also take the newspapers . . .’ toots the night mail in farewell.

‘Pah!’ growls the big Continental, ‘you may take the divorces, but I take the divorcees!’

‘I don’t think you’re quate nace!’ says the Streatham local, with a stiff look about her mid-Victorian smoke-stack.

‘Hear, hear!’ whispers the Orpington tank. ‘This boat traffic makes people positively . . . well, positively!’

‘Sir Percivale’ cannot retort, for his last steam has gone.

* * *

'No two engines alike . . . not two, sir, and I've been driving these last twenty years. Like women they are! They want fussing! You may make 'em in the same shed to the same design, but they come out different. Now 4040 is a proper old devil. I used to take her to Bournemouth every night, and this one, made the same year, runs like a sewing-machine, she does . . . like cream she is, soft and smooth. . . . Right away, Alf!'

With a prolonged hiss and a stealthy movement of connecting rods the great 'mixed traffic' backs out over the points, turns the table, and, with the green signals calling in the dark London night, puffs slowly out to take a train to Devon.

White and Yellow

THE Chinaman was frightened.

His face registered no emotion, but his hands trembled.

'No smokee opium, John?' asked the plain-clothes inspector.

'No opium upstairs, eh?'

The little eyes gazed from the blank yellow face. No, he said, in high-pitched protest, he had never smokee since policeman say it was no good—oh, one, two, tlee years long ago—and, oh, yes, he had been to the police-court once for having a pipe and having friends who liked to smoke it; but not now; oh, everything allee-lighty now. Honest. John no liar. . . .

The inspector flashed his torch on a dark, forbidding staircase, and expressed a firm determination to invade the upper regions. John was most upset. He assured us that nothing in the world could be more allee-lighty than his upstairs; but the inspector was not impressed.

First he took a glance round the basement of the queer rambling low-class café; room after room full of strange foreign men who backed away from us like a herd of startled deer. Some were clever at fading through curtains of sacking. One moment they were there, the next they had gone: a curious slinky business! There was an atmosphere of something suddenly stopped. There were swift chinkings as if piles of silver had been swiftly pocketed. It was pretty obvious that in this foul unfurnished den John made a good living from the rabble of foreign men who come to London in ships.

'Now upstairs with you, John!' said the inspector.

For one second John looked as though he would give anything for a long knife to twist in us; and the next he was all whispering humbleness before this rude invasion, back bent, hands spread, and over him the humility of an exile 'up against' the steel wall of an alien law.

'Allee-lighty,' he sighed, with resignation; 'allee-lighty!' and it seemed to me, the way he said it, that he was quoting Confucius!

* * *

I have inferred once, and I repeat, that Limehouse is the most overrated excitement in London, but when on the spot you can forgive most of the luscious things written about it, for it has atmosphere; it is a dramatic theme that just howls for a plot: a stage that cries for a drama. . . .

There was no light on the stairs. We went up by the light of the inspector's electric torch, hanging on a shaking banister, stumbling up the worn treads. Cobwebs and dust gave the place a moth-like mustiness. Like everything else in Limehouse, it was dreary, sordid, dirty, squalid. The soft moon of the police torch stimulated the imagination; one felt oneself on the track of Fu-Manchu; but by daylight how entirely nauseating it must be!

We stepped out on a dim landing with rooms leading from it. We opened a door. The inspector flashed his light over a chamber that looked ten thousand years older than the tomb of Tutankhamen, for dust had been falling for years over boxes, over a broken chair, over a collapsed table. The little window was boarded up with wood.

'You see ? ' said the inspector. 'You see ? '

The yellow light wavered over the tell-tale window.

The next room was the same, and the next: dark, musty horrors. In one was a dirty old iron bedstead without a mattress. No one had been to Paradise on it with a pipe for a long time, for each wire was thick with dust like a fall of soft brown snow.

'Allee-lighty,' whispered the voice. 'Allee-lighty, sir ? '

'It is all right,' whispered the inspector, 'for you can smell the stuff ten miles off.'

I was bored, and I felt sorry for the deprecating voice that followed us whispering in the darkness.

'Hallo, John,' said the inspector. 'This room's locked ! Open it ! '

John looked as though he might refuse.

'Open it ! ' ordered the inspector, raising his voice.

'That my room ! ' whimpered John.

'Open it ! ' repeated the inspector, with just a hint of handcuffs in his manner.

John drew a key from his pocket and fitted it into the padlock.

* * *

The room was lit by electric light under a pink shade. A fire blazed on the hearth; an electric radiator assisted in the uncomfortable warmth. It was a bed-sitting room, intimate, cosy, clean, comfortable, and refined. Indifferent pictures in heavily gilt frames covered the walls, a good carpet covered the floor. On a table in the centre of the room was a large bunch of grapes on a plate. A crowded sideboard bore a silver tray piled with biscuits and dates. Beside the tray were wine glasses and a bottle of Sauterne.

I took it in slowly, hit in the eyes by the crazy contrast to the decayed morgue of a house. The rest of the house was dead; this room was brilliantly alive.

I looked at John standing resentfully with his hand on the light switch, and knew that this room was his whole life. To make it he screwed money out of his compatriots and the sweepings of the Seven Seas in the dirty dens downstairs. So obviously was it his whole life that I felt I had no right to invade it, to bludgeon my way into a man's inmost secret. What right had we there, gazing as if at an animal's cage? I looked at John, noticed little refinements in the room, and felt that his eyes were as old as the world.

'Very nice, John,' said the inspector.

John made no reply.

Something moved. From beneath the bed walked a little Pomeranian dog. He stretched himself and yawned at us and sat down before the fire. Then light broke over me, and I began to notice all over the room evidence of a woman:

a neat pile of laundry at the foot of the bed, with three or four pairs of sand silk stockings on top, beside the hearth a pair of shoes, in the centre of the crowded mantelshelf the picture of a young English girl smiling. I looked again at the incalculable little wrinkled creature with his lean, monkey-like hand on the light switch and shuddered.

'Right. Lock up!' said the inspector.

The light flashed out, and only the firelight remained lighting the secret, playing grotesquely with the shadows in the live room of the dead house.

* * *

'All you can say,' said the inspector as we went through the dark streets, 'is that they treat that kind of girl better than many a white man would. They do, generally speaking, make good husbands. I believe it's going to rain. . . .'

Ambition's Road

IT is eight p.m.

The cinema at the corner has digested its uncritical queues. The billiard saloon is packed. Young men and girls enter the dance hall. Crowds gather for the second house of the music-hall. The lit streets are full of a vague excitement, an alluring restlessness, and through them pass young people with books beneath their arms. They are very ordinary young people. They look exactly like those who have gone to the cinema and the dance; but if you could see inside their heads you would, perhaps, observe a different point of view.

They arrive at a tall, ugly building situated in the centre of all the excitement. It lifts uncurtained windows into the darkness. They cross an asphalt playground and enter a place which by day is a London County Council school and by night a kind of monastery in which gather those pilgrims who have set their feet along the stern roadway of ambition. Twenty years ago it would, I suppose, have been called a night school, but to-day they call it an evening institute. It is one of about three hundred established in every part of London by the London County Council.

It is curious that London does not know the most interesting things about itself. It is possibly a penalty it pays for its size. I wonder how many young people who grouse about the lack of opportunity in their lives know that for a fee varying from 3s. to 15s. they can receive a year's instruction in almost any subject from book-keeping to foundry work, by way of Greek literature and dressmaking. Knowledge and the power to rise in life have never in the history of the world been offered to young men and women on such easy terms.

There is nowadays no excuse for any young Londoner to bewail opportunity; the opportunity is there for him to seize—just opposite the dance hall and the picture theatre!

* * *

You enter a room in which young men in the twenties are sitting at school desks, notebooks before them. The walls of the schoolroom are decorated with the coloured carrots executed during the day by London's younger generation! A barrister stands before a blackboard lecturing on commercial law. The students work in the City during the day, and come night after night to study the subject that will give them a 'pull' over the other fellow when the time comes.

In the next room tiers of young men and girls pore over Spanish primers. A pretty little girl holds her shingled head in her hands and reads in Spanish. The master pulls her up from time to time. It is all very much in earnest: a school that means to learn at all costs! A young girl comes in and says she's sorry she's late. She sits in the front row, takes out her books and pulls off her gloves. On her finger is a brand new wedding ring! You look at her and admire her, knowing how difficult it is for a young wife in a small home to do much more than run round the gas stove and wonder if the steak and kidney pie is burned again. . . .

The evening institutes contain hundreds of independent young wives who work in the City and pay fifty-fifty towards the home, and carry on with their studies at the institute, or else continue them as a hobby. Often, of course, a perambulator runs right across their talent, and—the Temple of Knowledge loses a priestess!

* * *

In the next classroom . . .

At dawn thy voice is loud—a merry voice
When other sounds are few and faint. Before
The muffled thunders of the Underground
Begin to shake the houses, and the noise
Of eastward traffic fills the thoroughfares,
Thy voice then welcomes day.

The girl stands in the centre of the floor and recites W. H. Hudson's poem to a London sparrow. Round her in a half-circle sits the class. She ends. The elocution teacher calls for criticism. The class pitches into the reciter. She did not stress this word or that, she did not give full value to that phrase or this. The teacher then pours balm on the hurt mind, and another student rises and recites, and runs the gauntlet of discussion. . . .

These young people are not going on the stage. They are learning assurance and the ability to express their ideas in public. Some of them will, no doubt (via Shakespeare and Milton) lead directors' meetings to victory in the splendid future !

'You cannot wonder that I am an optimist,' says the head master, 'for more young men and women are working to advance themselves every year ; in spite of the fact that every year outside attractions increase. It takes courage after a hard day's work to come here night after night.'

'The kind of courage that wins.'

'Exactly. And the kind of courage that develops character.'

You pass room after room, each with its small, intent class.

'It is wonderful to think that every night this goes on all over London,' says the master, 'not only in commercial institutes like this, but in technical ones, in laboratories and workshops, art schools, and so forth. Forty years ago the night schools taught under 10,000 pupils ; to-day the evening institutes of the London County Council are attended by 120,000.'

* * *

You go out into the busy streets where the omnibuses mass at the junction, where the crowds, free for a few hours from duty, move in search of amusement and excitement. You remember the quiet class-rooms, the young heads bent over books. You feel that perhaps London's proudest boast should be that when night falls she opens the road to Ambition to all those of her children with the grit and the nerve to take it.

Love and Youth

'MY dear!' he says.

'My dear!' she says.

Wonderful the way lovers meet in London every night as if the world had been born again that minute! You can see them 'under the clock' at Charing Cross, at the Piccadilly Tube—the meeting place of love and £ove—and you wonder, generally speaking, what she can see in him, how she can tolerate the way his tie rides up over his winged collar, and the cow-like glassiness of his eyes when he comes towards her in the crowd; such an ordinary little fellow.

'Where shall we go?' says Romeo.

'Mother says I must be in at ten,' says Juliet.

'Right-o. Let's go to Soho. I know a little foreign place where . . .'

It is Friday. In Romeo's pocket reposes the weekly packet containing four pounds in Treasury notes. Going to Soho will cut an awful hole in one pound, which in terms of knightly hardship represents, according to the Arthurian reckoning, the meeting of a knight with one dragon and two giants in an enchanted grove. (The grove is certainly enchanted!) They link arms and cross Piccadilly, where the red and the green and the gold lights wink, and they go down Shaftesbury Avenue, their souls suffused with the warm desire to link their fate with a furniture instalment organization.

Marriage seems to them the one reality. Everything else is just playing at living. Romeo aches to escape from his lodgings ; Juliet longs to escape from her home ; and to both of them the act of putting a Yale lock into the door of a red brick box represents a shattering victory against the ghastly forces that keep people apart. Romeo has dreamed of going home and finding her always anxious to greet him, her soul on her lips ; and Juliet has dreamed the slightly more practical dreams of women : how far ten pounds in the post office will go towards a white satin dress, new shoes and stockings, and things like that. It would be nice to be alone in her own home . . . no eternal nagging . . . no 'Now mind you're in at ten sharp, my girl' . . . no sisterly backbitings and cattiness ! Why can't people be happy together and kind to each other ? Marriage is the way out. . . .

(Ignorance and lack of imagination have been responsible for more fearlessness in danger than all the calculated bravery in the world !)

* * *

'Drink ? What shall we drink ?'

'A small lemon !' says Juliet.

'Come on. Let's have some wine !' whispers Romeo. One line in that wine list sticks in his imagination : 'Marsala, 3s.'

'Let's have a bottle of that !' he says, putting his finger on it.

The waiter droops off in a pale contempt.

They drink the golden error in large draughts like lemonade, and discover each other's feet beneath the table. It is that time when people like Romeo and people like Shakespeare feel that words are just bundles of old sticks snapping. He leans over the chicken *en casserole* :

'I love you ! ' he whispers huskily.

'Sssh ! ' she replies. 'Some one'll hear you.' She receives an impassioned hack on the ankle.

* * *

'Dangerous the ways boys and girls fall in love and rush into marriage, isn't it ? ' says a reflective person at a near table. 'Look at those two. What is he, do you suppose ? '

'Rather sweet, don't you think ? ' says the woman quite tonelessly.

'In a way—yes. They ask so little of life, knowing so little of it, therefore they may get more out of it than most of us. I believe they are the happy people. He will be quite happy all his life in a rut . . . can't you see him wheeling a perambulator on Sundays and clipping the front hedge . . . and she'll be happy round a gas cooker, rather damp about the forehead, but—frightfully happy ! '

'Awful, isn't it ? '

'I wonder. Nothing piles up more misery than an imagination ! '

* * *

Romeo pays his bill, and through a rich mist

of marsala comes the fact that he has paid away thirteen and sixpence. His mind automatically visualizes next Thursday as a cigaretteless day. (He owes his landlady fifty shillings !)

Through the star-spangled London night they go, hand in hand, on top of an omnibus. It begins to rain, but that is all the more wonderful, because they can pull up the oil-sheets and cuddle closer.

'When we're married,' he says reflectively, 'I shouldn't be surprised if I got a job with Wilkins's for four pounds ten shillings.'

The woman answers him.

'You stay where it's safe, dear.'

He does not recognize the ancient voice, being intoxicated with complicated emotions :

'D'ju remember when I spoke to you at the corner by the Plough ?'

'Cheeky ! I noticed your eyes then ! I wouldn't have taken any notice if I hadn't—straight ! Or lor, here we are ! Come in for a second and speak to Mother—please do !'

They pause half-way down the dark road and say good night. All their sacred moments are spent in streets, on the tops of omnibuses, in public parks. . . .

'You do, don't you ?'

'Course I do, silly. . . . Come on. It's after ten.'

* * *

Juliet's family is gathered in the kitchen : Dad in shirt sleeves and carpet slippers reading a newspaper, Mother knitting a vague object, Phyllis manicuring her nails, the bottles and pastes spread out on the table round a half-full bottle of invalid stout. In the middle of this Juliet is like a strayed fairy.

'So you've come at last, miss,' says Mum. 'Good evening, Alf. Where've you two been? Soho? Hear that, Dad? Soho! Wasting their money. I should think you want something to do. Take a look at yourself in the glass. I wouldn't like to come home looking as if I'd been pulled through a hedge backwards.'

Mother gazes acidly at Romeo, who, acutely indignant at the injustice of her insinuation, smiles feebly and makes some remark about the high state of the wind.

'You're a nice pair, I must say!' remarks Phyllis maliciously, polishing her nails with a gory-looking piece of white plush.

'Shut up, sis!' says Juliet, and the air is brittle with female repression; invisible swords seem to be swinging. Romeo twists his hat in his hands and says that he must be going. Insincere smiles follow him to the door.

'Just like her to take up with a soft ass like that!' He knows what they will say. . . .

'Oh, I love you, I love you!' cries Juliet behind the bead curtain in the hall, and he feels her mouth trembling. She buries her head in his shoulder and clings; then, suddenly, she pushes him away as a bar of light falls and a voice cries:

'Now, you love birds!'

* * *

He goes through the London night unable to analyse the situation, unable to see ahead, unable to detach himself and look down on himself and his motives and actions, conscious only that he loves her and that the night is more gracious because she lives, and that the stars above the chimney pots are not more lovely than her eyes above a golden glass. . . . Thirteen and sixpence ! That must stop, that wicked waste of money ! Life is serious . . . now !

The moon above London hides her face, having heard all this over and over again.

Omnibuses in Bed

THE last omnibus goes down the road with its weary cargo.

'All change!' cries the conductor at the end of the journey.

If you did not obey him, or, rather, if you were able to remain in your seat, you would be carried at high speed into one of the busiest scenes in the London night. You would arrive at one of the many L.G.O.C. depots which, between them, put four thousand red omnibuses to bed each night and make them fit to rise early in the morning to take London to work.

Holloway Garage is the largest garage in the world. The distance covered each day by its scarlet inhabitants is twenty-five thousand miles, or, as they point out at Holloway, 'once round the world'. Holloway has two peculiarities: a new day does not begin at midnight—as everywhere else in London—it begins somewhere round about five-thirty a.m., when the first omnibus trundles out into the dawn. Monday is never Monday till this happens. The second peculiarity is that Holloway does not know the meaning of the word 'omnibus'; they call them 'cars'.

* * *

The clock strikes twelve! The entrance to Holloway Garage is congested by 'cars' standing two by two. Their engines run, the lights shine over empty seats, the conductors look along the queue with a Tottenham Court Road and Oxford Street expression, anxious to hand in London's pennies and the unused tickets, the drivers lean over the steering wheels, tired after the race home. They come from every part of London. You look at their indication boards and see that they have been gathered from Crouch Hill and Norwood, Highgate and Crystal Palace, Shepherd's Bush and Camden Town.

The engines throb. Slowly the queue advances inch by inch into the night nursery of the red fleet.

* * *

Hark! Far down the road—that melancholy, empty Holloway Road—sounds an approaching omnibus. You do not notice it because two hundred engines are running; but the natives do! They hear that lone 'car' coming along, and they go out into the road to look for it, because there is something in the sound of it that tells them it is an invalid.

It limps up and joins the crew.

'What's wrong, mate?'

'Only the blinkin' engine blinkin' well conked on the hill and . . .'

Omnibus drivers do not love their machines, as ships' engineers and locomotive drivers love theirs, possibly because an omnibus driver's life is a daily philander with three or four different 'cars', and abiding love has its roots in steady companionship!

The driver dismounts, casts a look of hate at the bonnet, and goes off to relieve his feelings on an official 'running report'. Mechanics come up and investigate the case. A marvellous man called a 'shunter'—who is a kind of super London omnibus driver—takes charge. (The difference between a 'shunter' and a driver is merely that whereas a driver can drive his 'car' with the space of tissue paper between his wheels and the wheels of the next 'car', the 'shunter' can take an omnibus backwards through a drapery store without upsetting a pin.)

The invalid is taken to hospital. No crime is greater for a No. 3 than a show of temperament on the Crystal Palace Hill. That is a contemptible 'let down'. So the Bad Boy of Holloway stands in disgrace with the mechanics groping at his entrails, his wheels covered with bits of Brixton, his indication boards dirty, his floor thick with tickets; and when they find a bag containing half a pound of pork pie on the top deck all the Golders Green omnibuses veil their windows and look down their radiators in horror.

* * *

As the queue advances into the juvenile Olympia, men attack them outside and inside. The outside men fill up the oil and the petrol tanks, the inside men sweep out thousands of tickets. Then comes the murder gang.

They advance wearing gas masks. They carry syringes filled with perchloride of mercury. If any measly or mumpish child has travelled during the day this is the time the germs die. The 'car' then moves to a watery siding, on either side of which is a shower bath. Jets of water spray over the chassis, the windows, the top deck and the wheels. Cleaners polish the indication boards, the 'shunter' takes charge and insinuates the 'car' into the one and only position in the scarlet jig-saw from which it can make a graceful exit in its due order at five-thirty a.m.

* * *

It is interesting to 'board' an omnibus in the great nursery where they sleep and, sitting on the front seat, to take a look round at the red fleet at rest.

They stand, hundreds of them, berthed in the darkness, tremendously Londonish. I do not know any more typically London assembly except possibly a parade at Scotland Yard or a battalion of the Guards. The red omnibus is as characteristic of London as the blue policeman. Paris is a city of lunatic taxicabs and clumsy, single-deck Molochs like pirate sloops; Berlin used to be the city of the broken-down droshky; and other capitals have each their own mode of movement, but none, I think, quite so spectacular as our four thousand scarlet two-deckers. They, with pillar boxes and the Household Troops, provide that subtle touch of colour which we love; that line of scarlet against the silver-greyness of our rain-washed stones.

It would be an artistic calamity if the L.G.O.C. painted its 'cars' black; it would change the look of London. . . .

And sitting on top of a sleeping London omnibus at two a.m. is the ideal time to write. I will have one some day in a garden. All our best thoughts arrive on the tops of omnibuses. Sometimes one's whole life seems to have been spent on them in the Strand! Lacking these red monsters, what a wilderness London would be; north would not know south; Peckham Rye would be sundered from Camden Town, and Norwood would be to Colney Hatch as the Cape is to Cairo. The taxi-cab is an incident in our lives; the omnibus an institution.

In spite of it, the omnibus is not a lovable thing. Drivers never call it 'Kate' in secret or stay overtime to play about with the magneto. It has become the modern London gondola without enriching London with any romance. It is true that there is an awful mystery about those long-distance omnibuses which go through the streets bearing the names of foreign places unknown to man, awakening the ambition to travel, and planting fear in the hearts of the timid. Perhaps those lost Londoners who disappear from home might be discovered living quietly at Ball's Pond or under the promised oak at Honor. . . .

'Are you all right up there, sir?'

'Yes. I'm having a wonderful time!'

'Because we want to shunt her!'

'I don't mind.'

Who knows all the marvels of London till he

has been 'shunted' at two a.m. in the largest garage in the world, whose wheels never leave London, yet go right round the earth once a day?

Dining Out

'SIR IVAN, I think you will agree that Munchausen's theory on the pancreatic juices is—shall we say?—a trifle out-dated!'

Lady Anaemia Gasp crumbles bread with thin fingers and looks up with those bird-like eyes which have sought health in Bath, Aix-les-Bains, Cannes, Vichy, Contrexeville, Harrogate, Wiesbaden, Marienbad, and that awful place in Italy where they put you in a nightshirt and take you into the bowels of a steamy earth.

The pink candle-light glows over shirt fronts which conceal a little light indigestion, over faces on which self-pity and fear have etched fine and expensive lines. The silver shines into polished mahogany as if in still water. There sits Mr. Adolphus Quinsey, a famous neurasthenic who fears death every night (he owns much slum property), Mr. Green (liver), another distinguished invalid, the Dowager Countess of X (old age) and Jane Lady Boreington, who possesses more harmless symptoms of approaching death than any other woman on earth. What a curse money is!

An interesting party.

* * *

The great Sir Ivan, one of the world's foremost medicine men, sits at the head of his table and thinks as he dips the tips of his fine fingers into the finger bowl—who knows? What a fortunate thing that people's insides have not kept up with evolution? Lady Boreington's liver, for instance, has been worth a thousand a year for six years, and Mr. Green's kidneys are positive gold mines. They never die, these people who believe themselves marked down by the archangel; if they did, of course, nothing on earth could stop them. They linger richly on, which is all to the good. . . .

Sir Ivan was always too handsome to become an ordinary G.P. Not for him the rush to help humanity into the world at the behest of frenzied fathers; not for him the small two-seater and the complicated secrets of a garden suburb. No! Early in life he developed the ability to pat a neurasthenic palm in that manner which, when accompanied by a deep, soothing and intensely masculine voice saying: 'Dear lady, don't worry, we will soon put you right', makes rich women sing a man's praises from Dan to Beersheba and even further—New York, for instance.

(Few things are more important in the psychology of success than the praise of the right kind of women at the right kind of dinner-party.)

If you went to Florida or to Florence you would find some women ready to say with a gasp of ecstasy:

'Sir Ivan! That man is a marvel.'

And the funny thing is that they may be right!

* * *

As you sit and watch him you wonder how much of the charlatan and how much of the great man is behind that commanding, smooth, clean-shaven, noble exterior. Great men are so rarely handsome. Providence rarely hands out brains with beauty; and then there is usually something fishy about it! So that you sit fascinated by Sir Ivan, watching him as he methodically washes his grapes in a silver bowl, feeling that you are looking at a stage physician. He looks too good to be true. If you met him in an omnibus—which is not likely—you would at once say: 'That man is a great doctor!'

Personality is the most marvellous thing in human affairs. While Harley Street wonders, generally speaking, how to pay the rent and is too superior to join heartily in an epidemic, Sir Ivan gathers round him his faithful adherents, linked by that encouraging eye of his, that beautiful voice, those mesmeric hands. You feel that it is quite unnecessary for him to know anything about medicine; that such knowledge is almost a sad reflection on a man who is otherwise such a perfect gentleman.

'Oh, of course, Sir *Ivan* . . .' say his colleagues in the profession with a little wan smile and the accent on the Ivan. 'Oh, of course, Sir *Ivan*. . . .'

They infer that the man is a witch doctor, but that attitude, which seems to come under the head of medical etiquette, is to be expected. Success always breeds spite. However, they all call him in when heaven is at the other end of the stethoscope.

* * *

Into this shaded dinner party comes a young girl.

She has a notebook in her hand. All the guests look up and smile, for she makes their appointments for them. But she sees no one. She is agitated.

'His Royal Highness', they hear her whisper.

Sir Ivan rises. He apologises. He is very sorry, but duty calls him most urgently. Outside sounds the insistent call of a telephone. You look at him and feel sure that he is a real doctor. Some power has come to him. He looms above the lit tables, exuding confidence in the highest degree. You feel that if you were dying and he came into the room it would be like having a life-belt thrown to you. He is really marvellous.

He smiles, he thinks he may be back soon, he hopes his guests will play bridge upstairs, he bows, he goes, and with him goes the life of the party. Unless someone makes a move soon the conversation will turn to symptoms.

* * *

'His Royal Highness passed a good night, and there is no immediate danger.

'(Signed) SIR IVAN SMOOTH'

His disciples read the bulletin in the morning. Of course, there is no danger. Sir Ivan! That marvel. . . .

The 'Spring Onion'

'LET'S go on to the "Tadpole" or the "Spring Onion" . . .'

Every night in London there are people who 'go on'. They 'go on' because, like gamblers who cannot stop playing, they are wound up. They want that 'something more' out of an evening which is not there. Experience tells them that all they will get out of 'going on' is the feeling that they are wearing someone else's head the next morning, but—never mind—French sunshine bottled in 1911 is shining over their illuminated souls and . . . the 'Spring Onion' may be 'amusing'.

It is late. Piccadilly is settling down, its sound muted, its wheels fewer, its crowds less dense; and over that small triangle of disillusion formed by Shaftesbury Avenue, the Charing Cross Road, and Leicester Square is a dreary reluctance to go to bed, and the suspicion that many have no beds to go to. The beggar leans against the wall holding out a thin, hopeless hand, containing one box of matches; big limousines go by with lights that glow on grey cushions, furs, and white shirt fronts; little sharp harpies walk the pavements, while shifty, seedy young men in groups stand about as if lost or waiting for a leader. It seems to you that the clean tide of life has ebbed, leaving this queer driftage on the shore. . . .

The 'Spring Onion' is a night club. Night

clubs in London are of two kinds: clubs to which people go to spend money and clubs to which they go not to spend money. The 'Spring Onion' is that kind. As you leave your hat and coat there trickles down from some distant place the throb of a trap-drum and the tinkle of a piano. You enter a room full of people.

At first sight they look dangerous. You might think that they are waiting for the dope to take effect; a most unjust assumption, because they are only bored. A thin girl with a corrugated back leans forward, observing, through a monocle, the movement of dancers in the next room. Now and then someone waves a hand to her and she replies with a thin smile and taps the ash from her cigarette. A young commercial traveller from Sheffield sits opposite, believing her to be a vampire. Three young men with alcoholic puffiness at the eyes sit and talk together in loud voices, two or three smartish elderly men laugh loudly with their partners; in odd corners sit the evening dress explorers, the people who have 'gone on' in the hope that the 'Spring Onion' might be 'amusing.'

Amusing!

They glance round and conclude that they are in Bohemia. Quite a number of people hold the same belief.

'Almost like Paris,' says a stockbroker's wife as a young man with long hair goes by.

There are few things in Paris so honest; this is not a side show for trippers; it is a perfectly genuine home for lost dogs.

The atmosphere of the 'Spring Onion' is one of unrelieved sadness. It gets you at the heart. The louder they laugh and the longer they dance, the more it gets at your heart; for fifty per cent of the 'Spring Onions' do this night after night, month in and month out, because they are lonely and hate the thought of going back to furnished rooms. For a few shillings a year they can belong to the 'Spring Onion' and forget in drink at a reduced price that achy something at the back of their minds.

The clock goes round and some of them give it the quick, spiteful glance reserved for enemies. Only one-thirty! Oh, dear! Too early to go. Waiter!

They order poached eggs and whisky. They do not want the eggs, but after a certain hour eggs chaperone whisky.

So the small hours drift by.

The normal eyes of those prosperous merchants who have 'gone on' watch the scene without appreciating its essential pathos. They wonder dimly how much wickedness is behind it all; they feel that these people could not endure this dullness every night unless . . .

A pink-faced young visitor who has been mixing champagne with poached eggs and whisky, and feels himself filled with a pagan beauty, decides to put things to the test. He approaches the thin, pale girl, and says:

'Shall we dance?'

She adjusts her monocle and regards him slowly:

'We will not,' she replies.

The pink-faced young man retires, wondering why everybody looks game and won't play.

*   *   *

Under its elaborate pretence of cheerfulness is not the 'Spring Onion' the Club of Lost Dreams? Are there not people in London—in all great cities—who dare not be alone with themselves, who must seek company from loneliness, from things undone, from opportunities missed, from that demon which sits on guard at a man's conscience, making him cry: 'Go away! How dare you say I am second-rate? You know I have never really had a chance!'

*   *   *

'Then,' say the people who 'went on' next morning, 'we went to the "Spring Onion". Extraordinary crowd . . . oh, yes; *most amusing*!'

'Charlie Brown's'

YOU, who are possibly bored with the Berkeley, may care to dine with me at 'Charlie Brown's', just outside the gloomy gates of the West India Dock, East. . . .

We go into the bar to have a gin and Italian. It is full of ships' officers discussing the traffic of the Seven Seas. Through the folding panels of the bar, designed to hide the guilty face of the drinker from the barmaid, we see, opposite us, men of the lower deck drinking beer, as they also discuss the traffic of the Seven Seas! More people meet unexpectedly in 'Charlie Brown's' than in any other spot in London. We admire their sunburn. (A ship has just berthed with rum from Jamaica.)

However, we merely notice these people and forget them, for we are in a most peculiar bar. It looks like a junior branch of the South Kensington Natural History Museum. Queer stuffed creatures presented to Charlie Brown by the mercantile marine of every nation hang from the walls, crown the eminence of cupboards and repose dustily on the top of cabinets. Prominent among them is an unfortunately born calf with three times the normal allowance of legs. There are snakes in bottles (and, I am sure, someone's appendix), Chinese gods, Japanese ivories, African assegais, French bronzes, and, hanging from the ceiling, a long, dusty pipe which, sooner or later, someone will tell you ‘ is the pipe Billie Carleton used to smoke round the corner in the Causeway ’.

‘ Dinner’s ready ! ’ says a charming girl from the bar.

We go to the dining-room.

The room has a wooden roof. From this roof hang more curios. The bar was merely an introduction to this. Our eyes have time only to appreciate an albatross speared to the wall, and someone’s skull hanging from the ceiling, before we are led to large plates of roast pork and apple sauce. We sit at a table occupied by men with very clear eyes and very stubborn chins : young men round whose lounge-coat sleeves is the ghost of gold braid. (A ship’s officer can never disguise himself !) At the head of the table is Charlie Brown.

Now suppose you were a stoker in Shanghai and you said : ‘ I know Mr. Baldwin and Mr. Winston Churchill ’, no one would pay any attention, but if you said : ‘ I know old Charlie Brown ’, someone would at once stand you a drink—which would be the highest compliment one man could, in such circumstances, pay to another. Wherever ships go over the seas, in whatever harbours they rest, you will find someone who knows Charlie Brown.

Mr. Brown, who is sixty-seven years of age, is short and muscular. He has the figure of a man of thirty, the instincts of an artist, looks like a retired gladiator, and wears a peek-a-boo shirt and collar cut low at the neck to give him air. He ran away to sea when he was a lad, but hated it so much that he came home and settled down.

Then he developed the collector's instinct, and started buying beautiful things. His clients, with no real appreciation of Charlie's tastes, began to present him with bottle-nosed sharks and parrot-faced fishes, and shrunken human heads from the Cannibal Isles; which accounts for the queer appearance of the public rooms.

No man with a tinge of feeling could refuse monstrosities carried at great personal inconvenience from the other end of the world!

* * *

Charlie Brown explains his exhibits as we dine:

'That lifebelt up there came from the first German ship captured in the War . . . that skull is from the South Sea Islands. You wouldn't think the albatross was snow white underneath, would you? It is! They say an albatross can crack a man's skull with its beak.'

We gaze round at the dusty marvels. We avert our eyes quickly from things in bottles—from a small mummified baby in particular—and we appreciate the childish happiness of the tough fellows who brought these things across the sea to Charlie.

'That,' says Charlie Brown politely, 'is, I have been told, the pelvis of a lady.'

We look up and see a dusty bone hanging from the point of an antler.

There is so much else to see that we do not dwell on this pelvis as we should, or speculate whether it ever walked down Bond Street. . . .

'The pelvis of a lady.' What a perfect title for a modern novel!

'And now,' says Charlie Brown, 'if you've quite finished I'll take you upstairs.'

* * *

Here is probably the most surprising room in East London. In an ordinary front sitting-room Mr. Brown has crammed the results of forty years' acute collecting. Ivory and bronze are his passions.

An embarrassing display of Chinese and Japanese ivories stands packed in the room on tables, in cabinets, on shelves. There is a remarkable Louis XIV cabinet with painted panels, an 800-year-old Chinese cabinet, an Elizabethan prayer-book bound in faded embroidery, statuettes cut in the finest ivory of fishermen going out with cormorants to fish in the Chinese manner.

'Everything nice I see I go after!' says Mr. Brown, as he wanders round the room fingering his treasures with the loving fingers of a born collector.

He points out objects which the London museums would like. (Till a collector can do this he is a mere beginner.) We sign a visiting-book containing many famous names (which proves that fame is not always made in, but always spreads to, Mayfair), and then we take our leave.

* * *

In the bar downstairs the tankards are

replenished. The worthy fellows pour beer down knotted throats.

Some, no doubt, pledge themselves to bring Charlie back from the next voyage a pig with two heads, little guessing that when Charlie leaves his Barnum and Bailey dining-room he goes upstairs to enter the rarefied regions of art, to stand with his head on one side before a fifteenth-century statuette of Joan of Arc, and become quite a different Charlie Brown. . . .

Life is a queer, unexpected business, and 'Charlie Brown's' at the gate of the docks strikes a keynote.

Fire!

FIRE!

Through the London street roars the scarlet escape to the urgent clang of its big, brass bell. You have a second's glimpse of a man crouched over the wheel, 'riders' manning the escape, faces tense under burnished helmets, the long backward sweep of the rescue ladder; and you hear the crisp roar of an engine with the power of sixty horses in its voice.

It is poor, pale blood that does not tingle to this, the swiftest, most heroic pageant of our streets. It always seems to me, as the red cars cleave their clamorous way through still traffic, that I have seen a chariot and its heroes thundering, as in some ancient epic. . . .

Come with me to the head-quarters of the London Fire Brigade, and we will look behind the scenes of this drama. The time to go is at night, for it is then that out of the silence of London may come from anywhere the cry for help; at any moment that old enemy of London, the little red flame that licks and writhes and flickers, may leap up and illuminate the stage.

* * *

Brigade head-quarters, in the Southwark Bridge Road, reminds me of a battleship. There is a fine disregard for steps. Men swing down brass poles as sailors swarm down ropes, they shoot from the top floor to the bottom in a second. The men in blue look like marines; they have the competent, rough-and-ready smartness of seamen; the same humour.

A perpendicular ladder with brass-bound rungs leads to a kind of quarter-deck, and beyond is the most watchful room in the night of London—the telephone room of the G.H.Q. Fire. Men in uniform sit before the switch-boards. One is waiting for calls from London's 1,670 street fire alarms; another waits for the call from fire bells; a third has the general public's calls; a fourth is in touch with the other sixty-two fire stations in the County of London.

On the wall hangs an extraordinary map of London; it is London in terms of conflagration. Sticking in it are cork disks which represent the exact position at that moment of every fire engine and escape in the London area. A young fireman stands beside this map and keeps it up to date, so that the chief officer, coming in at any moment, can see at a glance how every fire-fighting machine is employed.

'Where's fifty-two and three?' says the superintendent, giving a quick glance at the map.

'Small fire in Chancery Lane, sir!' replies the map keeper.

As you look at this map and turn to this room with its listening firemen you have an impression of astonishing watchfulness, unsleeping, tireless.

'Could you have put out the Fire of London?'

'Well, it wouldn't have started had we been in

existence then ! We should have nipped it in Billingsgate ! '

Downstairs there is a card-index room like no other in London. Each card bears the name of a well-known building, and on it is written the recipe (in terms of engines and escapes) necessary for its extinguishing ! The whole of the great Oxford Street drapery stores are tabulated here ; you can look through the cards and see how much water power and how many ladders are necessary on 'the first call' from Jones and Brown's !

'Yes, something happens nearly every night.'

In 1925 something happened 7,476 times ! Those were the fire calls answered. The actual fires put out in London last year were 5,168.

* * *

You cannot talk long to an experienced London fireman before he tells you stories of the air raids, that dramatic chapter in the history of the brigade which should be written up and put on record.

'We could hear the Zepp unloading far off as we crawled in on hands and knees. A sheet of plate glass came down and cut the brass comb off my mate's helmet as if it had been butter ! I remember that night well, because that was the time I smashed my shoulder. . . . I felt myself falling. I was in a cistern full of water and printer's ink. I found my electric torch. There were two dead bodies in the cistern. The bomb had flung great slabs of concrete about as if they were cardboard. One slab had blocked the stairway. On the stairway huddled together, piled on top of each other were about thirty men and women, dead—killed as they tried to fight a way out from the fumes and the fire. I found a baby with its clothes cut from it—not burned, but cut —so that when I picked it up they fell apart. Its body was not even scratched. . . . Oh, yes, it was dead. . . . Nothing could have lived in that room when the bomb hit the concrete."

Each profession or trade has its jokes.

" You'd laugh like anything to see a new hand on his first real job meet a bit of live electric wire! It's our great joke to push a fellow under it so that it catches his helmet. He's wet through, of course, and that makes it worse for him! "

" What does it feel like ? "

" Well, at first you think an elephant's kicked you under the jaw! That teaches you! You watch out for hanging wire after that! "

* * *

Down in the station is the drama. . . .

The big scarlet escapes stand, bonnets to the door, rugs over the radiators, and beside each " van "—as they call them—the " watch " sleeps on camp beds. This is the first escape on duty. The men sleep fully clothed, their big boots beside the beds, ready to step into, their helmets on the " van." The same with the engines.

What happens when the call comes ? The men in the look-out room receive it and press a button.

Fire !

The lights leap up over the engines and the escapes, the fire bell rings, the men leap from bed into boots and jump to the 'van', the driver starts his engine, a pipe-clayed rope that hangs above the driver's seat is pulled, the doors swing open, and with a clang-clang-clang of the bell the first escape on duty is out in the London night.

Two seconds !

And more behind ! The next 'van' and engine are ready !

'Better be soon than sorry' is the unofficial motto of the brigade !

The men sleep wrapped in brown blankets like troops bivouacked on the eve of battle. Every night, and at any moment of the night, the dim station may blaze with light and sound, calling them from sleep to an inferno of flame, with a house reeling against a scarlet sky and, high up above the smoke, a life in peril. . . .

They sleep . . . always on the eve of battle.

Behind the Scenes

THE first night of a new play.

A second act has fulfilled the promise of the first. Over the theatre is that electric tautness, that marvellous feeling that every word is 'getting over' to the still rows of bleached faces in the darkness.

The author, who for an hour sat in the shadows of his box with the feeling that he was about to witness a child of his sacrificed on a heathen altar, now sits confidently in the front, the glow of light on his boiled shirt front.

A friend has just whispered that the libraries are making a 'deal', and that old So-and-So is ready to bet that 'the show will run for a year'. The author nods. That means that he will not only be able to pay all his debts, but that he can also go to the South of France, and never, never again have to say he is out when a man calls with an overdue account.

Wealth. Even in his preoccupation with his play he thinks how marvellous it will be to have not only enough to be miserably comfortable—the competence which illuminates unattainable desires—but . . . wealth.

Those much better plays, which no one would look at yesterday, can now be unloaded one by one! Funny place the world!

* * *

But the audience care nothing about him at this moment. Their sympathies are centred in a woman who moves across the stage in a beautiful gold dress. She is a beautiful gold woman with tawny hair and long, slim arms and wonderful hands . . . a new star.

She is struggling at cross purposes with life and in this struggle all the watching faces see mirrored their own tussles with life, so that they have taken sides with her against the other forces in the drama. Things are very real. While they ache for her success, and try hard to believe that virtue always beats vice, they can see only her failure, so heavily are the dice loaded against her.

She is not pretty; she is beautiful. Unsophisticated young men in the pit have already claimed her as their ideal, the unattainable. She for whom the world would be well lost. They do not analyse the spell that has been cast over them.

Here and there a very callow youth wishes that he might be brought into some heroic adventure on her behalf; a burning house from which, forgetting that he weighs only 8 st. 2 lb., he would swiftly and masterfully carry her . . . or a knightly rescue from a cynical man in well-cut evening clothes and a monocle, a rescue involving a fight, with those eyes looking on watching for his safety. . . .

She drops her eyelids and her voice. She concentrates the drama of the act into one swift second. The curtain falls. The storm breaks loose.

'Come round and meet her!' whispers the

author. His eyes are damp with unexpected happiness.

* * *

The dressing-room smells of scent and an electric fire.

An elderly suppressed-looking woman, wearing a neat apron over a black dress, moves round the room with a pair of silk stockings over her arm . . . those very gold stockings. A kind of overdue happiness lights her up. She walks in the reflected glory of success. She is the 'dresser'.

Three or four pink, elderly men perch themselves on various sofas, and when the door opens, as it does frequently, you can hear the muffled sound of the orchestra, feet pattering up stone stairs, and the hollow tramp of scene-shifters.

The men spring to their feet as the lady of the play comes through a side door, wearing a pink silk wrap edged with pink fluff. From the pinkness shoots a long bare arm, and she shakes hands. She seems smaller, and your eyes fix on her eyelashes, which are stuck together with grease paint.

'Billy, get me a drink, a very weak one!' she says.

The kind of man who is always discovered sitting on a chintz sofa leaps up and obeys.

Acting is a marvellous thing, you think, as you watch her, no longer the romantic lady of a dream but herself: a rather ordinary young woman. Unless you knew you would never guess that she could be a heroine.

'I'm famished,' she says. 'And I've had indigestion all day. I had kippers for breakfast.'

Her court make sympathetic faces. The elderly woman comes in with a gown over her arm and a pair of shoes. Outside somebody is shouting. The curtain is rising. . .

* * *

To the stage she comes again, radiant, cool, elegant. Her lovely voice falls on a hushed house. Each movement is followed by hundreds of eyes, each small gesture of fine hands.

You sit there, unable to feel that things are quite so real as they were . . . wondering if she had two kippers or only one.

Gladiators

'STOP messing abaht! Hit him!'

The cry rises from the crowded seats of the boxing booth. There is the same tone in it that told the gladiator in Rome to plunge his sword in the body of his opponent and—let them get on with the Christians! Stalls and circle are 'full up'. Eyes smart in the smoke of cheap cigars. Lights, green and spluttery, hang above the ring, and in the pool of these lights two East End boys are trying to fill each other's head with stars.

Their naked bodies are pink with the rash of the blows rained on them. Their hair is straight on their wet foreheads like the hair of Japanese dolls, their mouths sag, and their movements are becoming slightly vague: the brain and the nerves are not working together.

The fat seconds with their punched-in noses give twisted smiles, in which contempt for the clumsiness and admiration for the stamina of these young fighting cocks appears more or less evenly mixed. They are rather tired of swabbing them down at the end of each round, weary of inviting them to part with any teeth which appear superfluous; and they, like the fight fans, would be glad to see one or the other stretched on the floor.

Round fourteen!

It is curious at times to notice when two boxers

reach the last gasp that the subconscious mind functions even though the brain may feel like an underdone omelet.

Smack-smack-pat! goes a quick punch on the jaw of the thinner boy, and, more by good luck than skill he lands a blow on the other's nose which sends him reeling among magnificent constellations. Then, as this thin fellow recovers he flashes an incautious glance over the crowd as if in search of something, wipes the dank hair out of his eyes with a glove, and lurches to the attack. Just a second's lapse from concentration, but enough to show you that some part of him which yet remains unmashed is thinking of somebody or something outside the arena!

You have not far to look! Midway in a row of intent enthusiasts sits a girl who has evidently put on her best hat. She does not move. She just sits with wide eyes watching; and she is watching the thin youth. Every time he lands a crack at the other lad she tightens her hold on her handbag; every time the other boy lands a crack at him her lips part and her eyes go wider. . . .

'Stop messing abaht! Hit him!'

At that wild roar of the bored crowd she moves her shoulders and looks at the man next to her as if she would like to say:

'Shut yer mouth, you great ugly brute! How'd you like to stand up to that?'

She is very anxious. It is difficult to say whether she wants her boy to win at all costs or whether she would like him to lose in order to have him out of it.

Round fifteen !
There is some booing.

* * *

The two fighters square up.

They hug one another in sheer weary desperation till parted. Then they reel and stagger together. Their arms shoot out and each one receives a blow on the point of the chin. The crowd looks on as if it would like to take a hammer to them. Suddenly the stockier man goes to pieces.

The girl half rises in her seat.

'Oh, Jim!' she cries. 'Smash him one—now!'

Jim, at the sound of her voice, makes as though he would turn; as though he would dearly love to describe in her general direction a gallant gesture with his glove, as though he would, if the flesh were not so weak, place his thickened lips in a smile. In that second the smaller man comes up and deals a beauty which stretches Jim flat.

'One, two, three . . .' they count over his body. Then he rises. His pulverized face looks angry. He discovers his opponent in the semi-darkness in the mist in which he moves, and slowly, deliberately—for they are both half-dead with fatigue—he gets one in between the eyes. The other lad falls, crumpled, done for! They count him out!

The crowd sing a facetious song. They carry off the body. Jim limps down as if in a dream.

'Gentlemen, I now announce Battling Jones and Blue Peter!' cries a man in a dinner jacket as two heavy-weight fighters stride into the ring and smile down on their partisans. The crowd howls with delight. This is the big scrap! That other sparring match is already forgotten. . . .

* * *

Outside in the night the boy called Jim is carefully counting half-crowns by the light of a street lamp.

'I can't see too well! You count 'em, kid!'

'Thirty bob!' says the girl in a voice that means money is money. They both look pleased. Over the swollen face of Jim spreads in parts a wrecked smile.

'That's a bit of all right, ain't it?' he says, pocketing the money. They link arms, and as they go off into London it seems to you that there is about her the pride of all women for whom men fight in tourneys.

The Unborn Home

I SET off on a romantic adventure.

He is to be married in the summer, and he is building a small house in a northern suburb which he wished me to inspect because I have followed every stage of the comedy which has led to this, now running with the hare, now with the hounds, on his side one day, hers the next—but generally on hers. . . .

We came—after living on an omnibus for hours—to a remote, lost district on the very edge of London where the roads, still glutinous with country mud, have lately received that accolade of civilization—lamps. The little houses, pink, gabled and garaged, march down hills which but yesterday were wet fields full of cows and marsh-mallows. There are hundreds of such roads in outer London now; the very edge of that lake of life which since the invention of the steam engine has overflowed from London, linking village to village in one labyrinthine network of streets.

These houses, so new that they have not lost an air of having intruded, as if still apologizing to dead thistles, stand with a coy, bow-windowed surprise at discovering themselves so swiftly 'desirable' and 'freehold'; so soon drilled to stand shoulder to shoulder like red grenadiers on that recently wet field.

* * *

The Unborn Home

It was ten p.m.

We walked down the 'avenue', admiring the saffron, the blue, the pink curtains in the lit windows of drawing-rooms—so bridal, cosy, and intimate. (Mothers-in-law may have been inside, but there was nothing to suggest it.) We caught glimpses of chintz walls, brass lanterns swinging in 'lounge halls', and once we heard a piano and a little pale voice declaring that she was less than the dust beneath his chariot wheel. It was all so new and experimental and it would have been terrible to know that hate had any place or prospect behind that saffron glow.

'You're quiet,' he said.

'Yes,' I said. 'I feel two hundred and twenty years old.'

Then, half-way down the hill, we came to a place where the armies of occupation ceased. Here houses flung dark gables into the night. Their windows were blind and unborn. Over them was written the word 'Sold' in red type. On past the empty houses, and at the bottom of the hill we reached a series of excavations; beyond was the wet wild field with a white mist over it; all the stages in the history of colonization in one short road! Up from these ragged walls and dark pits Pompeian doorposts rose against the sky; there were foot-high mantraps and duckboards over the mashed cocoa of unturfed gardens. We searched till we came to an extensive ruin.

'This,' he said, 'is ours!'

We leaped a ditch in the dark.

'Here,' he said in the showing-off voice that

comes naturally to people who are building anything, 'is the front door!'

I saw two posts in the mud. We then came to a wall.

'The fire-place will be over there,' he continued, striking a match, 'and you walk out here into the lounge hall, which is going to have a decent stained glass window. Over there—where they've left that galvanized tank—we have the dining-room, and outside will be a loggia and the garden. It's difficult to grasp, but you'll be able to imagine it all.'

I thanked him for this flattery, and he gazed round with the eye of a seer.

'We mean to do this room in blue and saffron,' he remarked.

I stepped out of a puddle into another, and began to feel that I was locked in the grip of a great natural force—as, indeed, was true. He roamed about in the dark, visualizing his home.

'In a few weeks,' he said, 'we shall be able to go upstairs.'

I looked 'upstairs'; and the stars were smiling.

* * *

It came over me, standing there in the cold dark in this unborn home, that there should be some office in the Book of Common Prayer for the blessing of such places. 'Forasmuch as all mortal men be subject to many sudden perils, and ever uncertain what time these shall be met. . . .' It might begin like that before calling down all that is kind and lovely in life upon these brave places. . . .

'What are you doing ? ' I asked him.

'Burying a shilling in our front door—for good luck, you know. But I must jab the mortar down or someone will find it and buy beer with it.'

I also took a shilling and rammed it well down into the mortar.

'For Babs,' I said. 'She'll probably need the luck more than you. We can't tell yet.'

* * *

Then we went out into that inhospitable road, which was all the history of man's struggle with wet fields, and we saw on the crest of the hill—for it was nearly eleven o'clock—the little saffron windows snap into darkness and higher saffron windows leap to light. The brittle stars winked and moved, knowing everything, having seen everything. At the top of the hill I heard a small baby crying; but I don't think my friend did.

Chinese New Year

'KUNG-HI!'

In the dark arch of the doorway a Chinese lad, who shivered in his thin serge coat, bowed and smiled, whispering 'Kung-hi!' ('I wish you joy!') as I went in over a courtyard to the guest-room in the lodging-house of Ah Tack in Limehouse Causeway. It was eleven-thirty on February 12, and I had been invited to see the Chinese New Year in; for the end of the Twelfth Moon was near.

Ah Tack's hidden little house is the Ritz of Limehouse to all Chinamen who sail the seas to London. They all lodge with Ah Tack between voyages. In the kitchens hang queer fish and pallid chickens killed in a peculiar manner and instantly boiled; also quantities of pork. There are turkeys' tongues dried and powdered, a mixture which the Chinese believe is good for consumption. Ah Tack's is half empty now, because there are fewer Chinese crews about, but time was when he was always busy. Many of his guests have no money, but that does not worry him as it would worry the manager of the Ritz. He just smiles and looks impenetrable—which means that his expression does not alter—as he folds his hands and says:

'You come again, perhaps next year?'

And his penniless guest replies:

'Most assuredly, and then most honourable debt will be discharged.'

Off he goes. It may be years after, but the bill is always settled—now and then by a relative of the debtor! A strange hotel for a strange people. They seem to have such a marked sense of the unrealities; they seem to me to go through life with a waiting-room air as if conscious that they possess a return ticket to Paradise. . . .

I crossed the courtyard and entered the room. In all London there was no stranger scene.

Six or seven Chinamen sat smoking on chairs round an ordinary kitchen range. At the end of the room was a shrine which extended from the floor to the ceiling. It was made of red wood, and the central feature was a picture of Confucius. The sage sat in crimson silk gazing at this Limehouse kitchen, philosophizing above his thin, black, drooping moustache. Before him burned two tall garlanded candles. On either side of the candles were white flowers in vases, plates piled with oranges, washed and polished, and a big plum cake.

This room is the only temple of Confucius in London. On weekdays the shrine is used as a kind of sideboard, and the cat sleeps on it in a basket. Sometimes a Chinaman will put down his cigarette and sit before the altar, shivering and muttering things to himself—or Confucius—oblivious, apparently, of the cat and the empty beer bottle, which would take on possibly more trivial minds from God.

'Good evening,' said Ah Tack. 'I velly glad you come.'

He was in shirt sleeves, which seem the badge of his office, and he wore a black velour hat. He introduced me to his lodgers. We bowed stiffly, and smiled. Then Ah Tack took up a pewter teapot and poured out a drink for me into a wine cup. It was neat whisky.

You must realize that it was, I take it, an emotional occasion. The Twelfth Moon had but a half-hour to its wane. We sat watching the clock and sipping the fire water. The candles burned with a steady yellowness that brought out the crimson in the robe of Confucius. The cat walked in, took one look at the lit shrine, and went out again. The Chinamen began to talk in that clipped sing-song which I find most difficult to follow. They talked about Shanghai. They talked about New Year's Eve at home in China . . . shops closed for three days . . . lanterns in all the houses . . . cakes and fruit and flowers . . . Chinese crackers that went bang-bang-bang and covered the floor with soft red paper. New Year's Eve, the day that all Chinese debts are paid.

Ah Tack rose, as if sad memories stirred within him, and poured himself out another neat whisky!

The door opened, and two wizened little Chinamen came in as silently as blown leaves. They drifted up to the shrine and, whispering, accepted a drink. The clock ticked on. . . .

I began to feel (as Ah Tack solemnly toasted me every two minutes in neat whisky) that I was assisting at the service of some decayed priesthood: at a ceremony which had lingered on from remote ages. Scenes like this must have taken place early in Christian times, when the last priests of Thebes gathered to celebrate the resurrection of Osiris, hardly knowing the meaning of the things they did, giving utterance to the death rattle of a faith. It was like that.

It was uncannily solemn and deliberate. I wondered what they were really thinking, these expressionless exiles. I wished something would happen. I wished that they would show some animation. I watched the clock anxiously, feeling that when midnight struck something remarkable and dramatic would occur. Perhaps they would pray before the shrine. . . .

* * *

It was five minutes to twelve.

The cat came in, very annoyed at being kept up, and attempted to reach Confucius. Ah Tack went round with the alcoholic teapot. (I think we all looked fairly swimmy about the eyes.) Then midnight. . . .

'Happy New Year,' said Ah Tack, rising and removing his velour hat.

'Sin-hi . . . Sin-hi!' cried his guests, which means 'May joy be yours!'

Then Ah Tack advanced to the altar and took a knife. His guests put on their hats and sat down. Someone put coal on the fire. I sat watching Ah Tack's priestly back moving about before Confucius, and it occurred to me that it would not be in the least surprising if he suddenly offered up a sacrifice. These composed, deliberate faces affect one like that. Nothing would be surprising. He waved the knife in the air, put it down on the altar, and came towards me :

'Have a mincey pie ?' he said.

I took an admirable mince pie, and so did every one. It was full of anticlimax.

* * *

Ah Tack shuffled to the shrine and began burning brown paper.

'What are you doing ?'

'Making good luck,' he said. 'Much good luck.'

On each piece of paper was written a sum of money. He gave thousands of pounds to the flames, sacrificing, I suppose, to the God of Fortune.

After bidding every one good night and a happy New Year, I walked out into the cold, dead streets of Limehouse feeling that I had been to a rather sad secret society that was on its last legs and in urgent need of subscriptions.

The Happy Man

I WAS finding my way to Blackfriars from a region of warehouses on the other side of the river, and the tramcar was empty. It was about ten p.m. The conductor was singing down below in a deep and penetrating voice as he stamped his cold feet on the platform . . .

> Yes, sir, that's my baby ;
> No, sir, don't mean ' maybe ';
> Yes, sir, that's my baby now.
> Yes, ma'am, we've decided ;
> No, ma'am, we won't hide it ;
> Yes, ma'am, you're invited now . . .

It was a singular voice—deep, full, ripe, and rather wild. He had a great sense of rhythm, and the stamping of his feet kept time to the dance tune. I was certain that he was having a good time all by himself on the platform as the tramcar spun on down the dark roads, on either side of which warehouses frowned with an air of locked strongholds. In a few moments he came jingling upstairs into the empty car still singing . . .

> When we reach the preacher I'll say . . .
> *(Where to, guv'nor ?)*
> Yes, sir, that's my baby ;
> No, sir, don't mean ' maybe ' . . .
> *(Threepenny, sir ?)*
> Yes, sir, that's my baby now. . . .
> *(Blinkin' cold, ain't it ?)*

'You,' I said enviously, 'seem almost horribly happy.'

'Happy?' he cried in a cavernous voice. 'What's the good of being anything else? We shall soon be dead. We all go the same way home. I've got no blinkin' reason to be happy; but I can't help it.'

'You are happy in spite of yourself?'

'Yes, and I've just had a rare old ticking off, too.'

'Why?'

'Whistling. You wouldn't hardly believe the dirty tricks the public serves you at times. I suppose some crusty old bloke was trying to read his paper and the tunes I was whistling got on his nerves. Well, why couldn't he have told me so? I'd have stopped! Instead of which he goes home and writes a stinking letter to the Tramways Department giving my number and complaining that I upset the whole car.'

He swung his satchel round till the pennies rang together indignantly.

'That,' he remarked loudly, 'was not true . . . in fact, it was a rotten lie. I never have upset the whole car—not the whole of it! Often people say to me as they get off: "Well, I wish I felt like you do!" and once, guv'nor, I had the whole car whistling! I did—straight! And what do you think got 'em? "Marchin' to Georgia." It's a tune, that is! Know how it goes? . . .

Bring the good old bu-gle boys, we'll sing ano-ther song.
Sing it with a spi-rit that will start the world a-long,

Sing it as we used to sing it fif-ty thousand strong
WHILE WE WERE MARCHING THROUGH GEOR-GIA.

'Great, ain't it? Got a swing with it! Better'n all this fox-trot muck that you whistle just because you can't forget it! When I told the missus she said, "Joe," she said: "if you don't watch out you'll get the sack"; and I believe she was right!'

* * *

I looked at him and realized that he had a certain quality. He was small and stockish, and his issue coat was made for a much taller conductor. He was one of those people who give you an impression that he ought to be on the music-hall stage; he was like a caricature of his calling.

He had a likeable personality, a gentleness of eye which was discounted by the gruff voice of the giant which is so often imprisoned in small men. I had a vision of him in his right environment; a little, slightly pathetic figure in the spot light of a large stage singing to a hushed theatre. . . .

'People often say I'm rude,' he volunteered, 'especially old ladies. And I'm not rude; it's the way I speak; I can't help it. Wish I could! Might be an inspector! But if I was to say, "Tickets, please"—just like that—somebody'd write up and complain about it. Straight they would!'

A girl got in and sat down.

'Where to?' bellowed the little man.

'Elephant,' she replied.

'You're only going the wrong way. Do you mind?' boomed the conductor in his terrifying *basso profundo.*

The girl looked a bit frightened and rose.

'Wait till I stop the car!' he shouted gruffly. It was a kind thought, yet the passenger appeared offended. I realized that the little man was one of those people born to be misunderstood, fated to suffer for a manner over which he had no control. (A touch of personality is also a disconcerting thing in the humdrum of life!)

'It's not often I can have a word with people like this,' he said, 'and I like talking. You're not an actor are you?'

'No,' I replied, 'I write.'

'Do you?' he said surprised. 'I should think you need a head to write. I've often thought I'd have done better at something else. It's not much of a life running up and down stairs punching tickets. I don't like doing it. . . .'

'Then why do you do it?'

(A silly question, put on purpose.)

'S'truth!' he cried, with deep feeling, 'I've got three kids! How many blokes are in the wrong job because they've got kids? Millions! And glad to be in any job! 'Course it's worth it! I got three fine kids: laugh and whistle all day long, they do; just like me. My missus says that between us we shall drive her barmy, but that's only her way of putting it.'

I smiled at the little lost artist, and saw him at home tumbling about and acting, putting all the vitality which he might have flung across the footlights into a rough and tumble on his kitchen floor. . . .

* * *

We swung in over Blackfriars Bridge, and the delicious curve of the Embankment lights swept on into the dark.

A new audience stood waiting innocently in the tram shelter, some for the stalls ; some for the gallery upstairs.

'Good night and keep smiling ! ' I cried.

'Can't help it ! ' he said. 'Yes, sir, that's my baby. No, sir, don't mean "maybe" ; yes, sir, that's my baby now. . . .'

His song was suddenly cut off, as an inspector emerged from the shadows. I heard his deep voice encouraging his audience to 'hurry along there. . . .'

I found myself smiling and quite surprisingly cheered-up.

Sorting the '5.30'

I THINK the grandfather of all good journalism, Daniel Defoe, remarked that nothing gave him a more vivid idea of London's size than the daily business at the Customs House. There was, of course, no G.P.O. when Defoe lived. I would give anything to show him round King Edward's Building, E.C., at about 6 p.m. any night of the week, for here the size of London leaps at you till your head goes round. . . .

It is nearly 6 p.m. All over the City of London those little enamelled discs—'Next collection, 5.30 p.m.'—have been removed from the pillar-boxes. The big evening mail has gone! It is the boast of the Post Office that letters posted before 5.30 p.m. in E.C. are delivered in the London area the same night. It is the rush mail of the day; a mail that comes in like a white avalanche, is stamped, sorted, broken up and sent out at once to flutter like an evening snowstorm over London.

In a long, high room 1,300 men grapple with the '5.30.' As you enter you push through an army of postmen who have just emptied the pillar-boxes and are handing in their enamelled discs and the keys which unlock the boxes on their 'walks'. (A policeman calls his patrol a 'beat'; a postman calls the same patrol a 'walk'.)

You go on into the most quietly efficient scene in London.

Sorting the '5.30'

Wide, travelling bands covered with letters and postcards empty a stream of correspondence into baskets. They travel from the post-boxes outside the G.P.O. As soon as a letter is posted it moves on and falls into the stamping-room.

Men carry the baskets and pour them into the general mail that lies like a miniature Switzerland on a series of long tables. It has come from pillar-boxes in office and street. The letters are arranged with the stamps all facing one way, and are passed through a machine that goes click-click-click, stamping 1,000 items a minute, writing 'British Goods Are Best' on the stamp, and adding a circle containing: 'London, E.C. (the date, the year), 6.15 p.m.'

'But this is a 5.30 mail! Why do you stamp it 6.15?'

'Collections are stamped three-quarters of an hour later than the pillar-box time because we discovered that some people got up to all kinds of trickery. At one time it was quite common for people to hear the result of a race sharp on posting time, write out a bet and rush to the pillar-box, and afterwards produce the postmark as a proof that they made their bet before the race was run! Things like that!'

One stamping-machine deals exclusively with official matter. Is there a more melancholy sight in the G.P.O. than 1,000 long buff income tax letters being rushed out with indecent haste to the, as yet, unsuspecting public?

The mail, stamped, passes on down the room in a steady stream, where it is joined by another stream of letters from dozens of provincial mails that happen to arrive at the same time. It is 'broken up'. It is sorted. Hampstead's letters go into one department. Norwood's into another. Park Lane's into a third; and so on. Postmen in the E.C. 'walks' come along, take up their bags, and go apart to sort the mail in the order in which they will deliver it. They make little piles, each pile a different street, arranged numerically. No two postmen sort their letters alike. They know their 'walks' and they know the peculiarities of them.

'Why do you put letters for No. 32 crossways on those for 46?'

'Well, you see No. 32 has moved to 46, and the housekeeper at 46 takes them in for him. No. 3 in C—— Street has a brother at No. 104. He's ill and has transferred his business to his brother, who takes his mail. Now see this! This is what makes a lot of trouble to us postmen. "Mr. Jones, Splendiferous House, E.C. 1." Now Mr. Jones has a little office in the roof, but he won't put "Room 510" on his notepaper, because he wants people to think he owns the whole blinkin' show. Till you get to know these people with large addresses and small offices you spend hours finding them. But you soon get to know them!

* * *

Past the crowd of sorting postmen (who seem to be playing some obscure card game by themselves), you go to the last scene of all. Outside in a great yard the Royal Mail vans await the first bags for the district offices. They are flung in, checked, the doors bang:

'Right away, Bill!'

And off the red van goes with income tax notes, letters beginning, 'Sir,—We are surprised to learn that the enclosed account . . .'; letters beginning, 'Dearest,—It seems a century since I saw you . . .'; letters beginning, 'With reference to yours of the 18th ultimo . . .' (millions of those!)

'Have you any statistics about the 5.30 mail?

'We have,' says the official, bringing out a book.

'An average posting every day for the 5.30 at this office is 146,395 letters, 3,983 postcards, 5,715 registered letters, which with newspapers, packets, etc., makes up a daily total on one collection of 260,280. But that is not the heaviest mail. Every week the 7.15 a.m. delivery in the City of London totals 6,642,700, and in addition . . .'

'No more figures, please! They cease to mean anything!'

'And remember that this is only one office.'

* * *

Upstairs you enter the region of foreign mails. Men are sending a few hundred thousand letters to Cuba, to Egypt, to small republics in South America whose names remind you of geography primers. In one corner of this room the whole

British Fleet is mapped out in little boxes, each box the name of a battleship.

'Admiral's Letters' is a big sign over this department.

'The admiral,' it is explained, 'being a big pot, has his letters delivered in a special bag.'

Downstairs again.

The clock strikes 7 p.m. A change has come over the big room. The white flood has ebbed. You have to walk two hundred yards to catch sight of its tail disappearing into the sorting boxes. Outside is a roar of motor engines and a slamming of doors. Postmen are shouldering bags and marching off into the night. The great room in the G.P.O. has digested the '5.30' prompt to the minute!

Then . . . click-click-click . . .

The stamping-machines all sing together. The busy 1,300 form up behind the tables. The revolving bands again shower their burdens into the baskets, hundreds of bags are again emptied on tables.

'That's the 6.30 just beginning!'

The tables are suddenly white once more! In a secluded corner a man who combines the eye of a hand-writing expert with the mind of a detective shuffles the casualties of the night mail:

'Mr. Jones, London.'

He flings it wearily into a box marked 'Blind'.

* * *

And the white avalanche of the 6.30 moves on through the machine. . . .

The Thames: Two a.m.

'ON a June night,' said the sergeant, 'this job is all pie, but just now unless you wrap the oilskin round your back—excuse me, sir, that's better—you're liable, if you don't mind me saying so, to catch a chill on the liver.'

The patrol boat of the river police shot out of the black shadow of London Bridge and nosed like a swimming rat to the Southwark side, where grim warehouses and wharves go down to the water. The sergeant sat in the stern, a river policeman beside him, and the driver crouched amidships over his motor, interested in the chug-chug-chug that told him whether it was running well or badly. The navigation lights bobbed and danced as we rode at full speed across the wash of a tug. . . .

'On a June night,' repeated the sergeant, 'it's just pie, this job, lovely and cool with sometimes a moon round as a soup plate over the Houses of Parliament so bright that you can see to read the paper. It's true that bodies are worse in June, but—there's always something, isn't there? You can't have everything all your own way, can you?'

He gave the grappling irons a push with his foot and they returned a gruesome rattle . . .

To our left the great drums of London Bridge, like the bastions of a fort, thrust their wedges into the swirling eddies of the river. The Thames is still strong here, as it was when old London Bridge was a place for wise men to pass over and fools to pass under . . .

What an aloof river is the Thames! It 'keeps itself to itself'. It never joins in things as the Seine joins in the affairs of Paris. Modern London has not tamed the Thames as some cities tame and domesticate their rivers; it is a melancholy, primitive streak in the character of London. The Embankment civilizes it for a few yards, but the essential wildness of it crops up at Westminster, where, it seems, rushes might grow on the slightest provocation, and, east, beyond Blackfriars, where the gloomy buildings stand with their feet in the water looking much as Thames-side buildings have looked since Augusta.

Yet if you would know London it is necessary to sail at night with the patrols of the river police, for it is then possible in an impersonal drapery of night really to see London; an experience that cannot happen by day. All you see by day is a muddle of roofs and streets and spires. From the old unchanged Thames at night the outline of London looks much as it always has looked, and by slightly closing your eye you can see first Augusta, then the Conqueror's London, then the London of the Middle Ages, then the London that disappeared in the reign of Charles II, each passing across your imagination in a kind of dark, exciting procession.

* * *

It was past midnight as we chugged towards

The Thames: Two a.m.

Wapping. We nosed round the hulls of tall ships, shining our lanterns over them.

'Bananas and tomatoes!' said the sergeant, indicating a galleon.

We came to another one:

'German! Full of reparation goods!'

We swam in under the shadow of Limehouse, every second revealing a narrow slit of riverside that seemed staged for a dramatic crime; steps awash in the tide, a cold lamp shining over them, and at the back shuttered houses. We criss-crossed to the other bank and came to a queer fleet at anchor:

'The smallpox boats,' said the sergeant. 'They are always fitted up ready to take patients down to the isolation hospital in the event of an outbreak.'

They were queer, old-fashioned craft, with tall smoke stacks and paddle wheels. Lower down the river we came to another flotilla. It was made up of Thames tugs, about thirty strong, riding at anchor side by side. This is where they hull when their day's work is done.

'Lights out!' whispered the sergeant suddenly. 'Let her go!'

He had seen something! The little boat shot ahead over the water. We overtook a man in a small rowing boat.

'Where's your light?'

'Got no matches!'

'Got your papers?'

'Yus.'

'Let's see 'em!'

Heads in peaked caps bent over the papers in the moon of an electric torch. More conversation about lights.

'Right! Let her go!'

Off we sped again.

'Can't be too careful about people who move in the river without lights,' explained the sergeant, 'but thieves aren't as bad as they used to be. There was a time when they'd have untied a loaded barge and walked off with it!'

We sailed round clusters of barges laden to the brim, lying together out in the stream with no one on guard. Then we turned and ran with the tide back to London Bridge.

* * *

One of the loveliest glimpses of London I have ever seen is that which unfolds itself at night through the jet black arches of Blackfriars Bridge . . . the pin points of the Embankment lights curving round to Westminster across an oily expanse of Thames, the lights wavering in the water, and in the background, grey and sleeping, the tall buildings of the Embankment . . . a little oblong yellow tramcar moving slowly in the darkness. . . .

Again, at Waterloo Bridge there is a marvellously effective view of that needle which had nothing to do with Cleopatra framed in the sweep of an arch. . . .

We shut off the engine and drifted. Someone arose and flung out a thing like an anchor that splashed and sank. Then he threw out something else:

'That first is the drag, and that other is the trip line.'

And there you must leave us—for it was not nice, in all that loveliness of London by night, to be drifting with the tide dredging, and talking about a lost woman. . . .

Big Ben struck two, and his great yellow face was like a friendly moon in the darkness.

Bloomsbury

THEY dine with the blinds up. Beyond the yellow oblong of the window is the darkness of the Bloomsbury square, with its skeleton trees beneath which the cats have their loud love affairs. . . .

The major dresses for dinner. He enters the Victorian room, making blustering, throaty noises and spreading a full-blooded heartiness due to an expensive-looking complexion, inherited, with a series of mortgages, from his family. He takes his seat beneath 'The Monarch of the Glen', and the critical eye would find an aptness in this; for he himself is the monarch of this glen, the arbiter of its fluctuating manners, the focus of its social aspirations—the star turn of the boarding-house.

Some people, knowing that his income from all sources, with the exception of the Turf, is two hundred and fifty pounds a year, would be inclined to laugh at his grand manner and put him down as a silly old snob. We will not. When an exile tries to re-create the atmosphere of his native country in a strange land no one calls him a silly old patriot; the major, exiled in the wilderness of poverty, is merely trying to remain true to his blood. He is not always successful except in the evening, for a dinner suit generally acts on whatever breeding there may be in an Englishman, just as it seems to obstruct the decent instincts of some nationalities.

During the day the major has vague dealings in saloon bars with foxy little men who live on horses, and at such moments, in his seedy bowler and his faded, pre-War, over-cleaned basket-weave lounge suit, you might mistake him for some not too honest camp-follower of Chance. In the evening, however, he reverts to his instincts: he is the perfect gentleman—Major Gorey-Goreish, D.S.O., of the 5th Royal West Blankshires (Princess Augusta's Own).

* * *

One by one the chairs are occupied. There is a clatter of plates. A small, sour girl who seems to have been weaned on disillusion emerges from a Japanese screen bearing a trayful of steaming soup plates. She rests the tray on her knee as she unloads soup to the people whom Fate has brought together in Bloomsbury.

'Pea soup again!' whispers a shaggy young man at the end of the table.

He looks across for approval to a pale girl with a sleek brown head; but she takes no notice. Stuck-up lot in this place!

'And when I was A.D.C. to Lord Bloodsome in '95,' booms the ripe voice at the end of the table, 'I met the Crown Prince in Ceylon, and he said to me . . .'

'Could you lend me fourpence, you dear old top . . .' mimics the shaggy young man to his neighbour with a furtive glance at the major.

'Really, how interesting . . .' remarks a faded widow as she crumbles bread with fingers which look somehow naked. Her diamonds went one by one years ago, after dear Arthur's creditors had been partially satisfied. Bloomsbury is full of faded ladies with omnibus clothes and a Rolls Royce air, who, after flinging possessions at the creditors of their husbands as one throws things to a pack of ravenous wolves, escape into discreet poverty with a carriage clock and a photograph of the Italian garden.

* * *

A young American 'Commercial' looks round at the well-bred derelicts and finds his worst suspicions of the effete English more than fulfilled. A lot of silly old snobs! He could buy them all up and write them off on his expenses as 'car fares', and no one would know. A bunch of bum failures without a dime between them, dressing up for dinner and talking about the foxes they killed years ago. Gee, they cut no ice with him! What a bunch of stiffs!

The shaggy young man who has just come up to London from the provinces and is doing quite well in the City, is inclined to agree with the American, with whom he has developed a spiritual affinity. 'Unmatey' gang, that bunch of the major's—probably he isn't a real major! Every time the young man smartly pierces a piece of Gorgonzola and marvellously introduces it into his mouth on the point of a knife he discovers the major's baleful eye on him! It is as if someone has whispered 'Bounder!' And he is not a bounder, but he hates to be made to feel inferior. He is annoyed at the major's ability to make his hands feel red and large. . . .

'Punk lot of goats, ain't they?' whispers the American.

'Yes; listen, now we're going to hear for the twenty-third time since last Friday that ruddy story about Lord Dash and the wild pig!'

'Gee, this is just fierce! Doin' anything to-night? Let's get clear of this and go up west.'

* * *

In the middle of the table a young man who is supposed to be something in the City looks on at the tragi-comedy, taking no sides, seeing both so well. (It is almost a pity to spy on them and put them in his play.)

He is as amused by the arrogance of the young hustlers as he is by the arrogance of the major with his aura of caste. The young men are going up the ladder of life arrogantly; the others are coming down in the same frame of mind. They cling pathetically to old things. Their 'air' is a barrier of self-protection erected against a social abyss. Having a tradition, they owe more to that tradition than to themselves, which explains the sting in the genteel poverty. They are also malicious, full of suspicion, soured by disaster and made mean by having so little—watch their faces when they are playing bridge at threepence a hundred. And with it all they are extraordinarily gallant.

Night by night goes by and the card tables are brought out. One by one the people who have known better days steal off to bed. What dreams come to Bloomsbury every London night no man can say, but it seems reasonable to suppose that the cats in the square often awaken faded ladies from Italian gardens to a grim little bed-sitting-room where a fallen carriage clock ticks in a patch of moonlight. . . .

The 'Old Vic' ⸙ ⸙ ⸙ ⸙ ⸙

THE man next to me was smoking a hearty little cigar. He may have been a plumber or a gasfitter or a carpenter; he had carried with him the careless atmosphere of one accustomed to bang about homes with a hammer.

'This is going to be a bit of all right!' he remarked, waving the stump of his cigar towards the stage.

Round us curved the gallery of the 'Old Vic'. It was packed with men, women, and children who had paid fivepence to hear *Aida*. Most of them were artisans, a few were labourers from the Waterloo Road district, and many were young girls and boys with more brains than money. There were three or four plump matrons sitting together eating cake as they waited for the curtain to rise.

'I remember this theatre thirty years ago—and more,' said the man with the cigar. 'Regular blood bucket it was in them days. A couple of murders in every act, and dead baronets all over the stage, and the gallery trying to throw things at the villain. . . . Now, of course, it's a real theatre. You get something to think about here. . . . Shaw's clever, of course, but he doesn't touch your heart. I like Yourip-ides. And I like opera, although I couldn't abide it at first. But I stuck to it; and now you can't keep me away. . . .'

The lights were lowered. Instantly the full theatre was hushed, and there fell a dead silence of people who have come with the grim determination to extract each hard-earned pennyworth of enjoyment or instruction.

Radames stepped forward and sang that sweet cruelty to tenors, 'Celeste Aida', and I could see by a glow that my friend was softly beating time with his cigar.

* * *

I will say just this of *Aida* at the 'Old Vic'. It was the most heroic show I have seen in London. A small stage, a small but marvellous orchestra, beautiful lighting, inoffensive scenery, and this great spectacular opera, which ought to be performed in the Stadium, 'got over'.

I live in hope that some day a producer will buy a book on Egyptology and dress the opera correctly, for nothing could be more effective no matter how small your stage. Someone deserves praise for putting on Pharaoh's head the red and white crown of Egypt; surely the first time this has happened in the history of the work!

* * *

The curtain fell on Act I, and the gallery went mad. Fancy an English gallery whistling, stamping, and yelling with joy at an Italian opera! 'Oh, this is nothing,' said the man with a cigar. 'When we like a thing we let them know about it!

He then told me that when the bombs were dropping round Waterloo Station during the War the 'Old Vic' audiences sat listening to Shakespeare night after night. Macbeth had to raise his voice to carry it to them above the fire of the anti-aircraft batteries!

* * *

I explored the dress circle.

It was packed with people from every suburb in London. So were the stalls and the pit. In the interval I went downstairs and joined a great crush round a huge coffee urn. Here I met Chelsea in art silk and Balham in a serge costume, also the masculine counterpart of each.

'Isn't it great?'

A young man who was eating a substantial cake asked me had I ever heard *Aida* before? In any other theatre I might have said 'Yes', and have left it at that, but here I told him what it is like to hear the opera in Egypt in the opera house for which Verdi wrote it, and afterwards to go home through moonlit streets with the tall palms rasping in the Ezbekeyih Gardens.

As I listened to the crowds talking I gathered that the 'Old Vic' is a kind of compromise between a theatre and a club. They knew each other. They knew the actors and actresses. They had ideas about finance and production. A girl sold me a copy of the theatre journal as people at a church bazaar sell you the parish magazine. On the front page I read that: 'Early in Birthday

Week [Shakespeare's] some kind member of the audience brought great branches of rosemary from the country and filled the various offices with it because it was a *Hamlet* flower. . . .'

Does any one ever feel such affection for any other theatre in London ? Has any other theatre the life and enthusiasm this playhouse has ? I began to revise my ideas on the National Theatre !

* * *

In the gloom of Waterloo Road I passed my friend of the cigar. He was whistling most of the last act with tenacious enthusiasm, and I am perfectly certain that he will go on whistling it as he mends burst boilers, or looks after the bathroom taps, or carves out cabinets.

The 'Old Vic' is London's one dramatic inspiration.

The East's 'West End'

LONDON may mean anything to a man.

To you, at home in a club chair, with Mrs. Browne sitting opposite, and the children asleep in the nursery, it means one thing and . . .

The squat timber ship, heavy with a small pine wood from the Baltic, comes rolling round North Europe with the salt caked to her smoke stack and the cook's cabin flooded. Now and then it seems that she vanishes in the sweep of the sea as if sucked down, her bridge heels over into the angry greyness but, bit by bit, with a kind of desperate persistence, she makes headway, and, in time, discovers the mouth of the Thames. She steams into Limehouse Reach, and slowly, for she is very tired, berths in the Surrey Commercial. There is a great rattle of chains, and—one more cargo has been brought to London Town!

A hefty Scandinavian sailor looks at the twinkling chain that is Rotherhithe Street, and feels glad that he is in London once again. His tow-coloured head cropped up quite early in English history, and those bleak blue eyes looked first at England over the poop of a viking galley. He is the same man who gave Alfred the Great much trouble; and as he looks at the lights of Rotherhithe his eyes are much the same as they were when he contemplated a raid on East Anglia—but perhaps we are imaginative!

One fact is certain; the London night calls

him! He wants to be ashore jingling money. He receives an advance of pay, and, with a gay whistle, is soon slouching his six feet two of blonde manhood through the grim darkness of the docks, where stark cranes stand in rows outlined against the faint, smoky gold of a London sky.

* * *

He is in London!

He likes London! He tells people at home about London, the greatness of it, the warmth of it, the excellence of it when you have been rolling in from the Baltic with salt on the funnel and the berths awash! A great place London!

He whistles through Rotherhithe Tunnel and enters that region of the Swede and the Dane—Shadwell. He goes on through dark streets which smell of fried fish and fried sausage, he passes entries where pale little girls whisper to him, but, being a northerner and not a southerner, he walks straight on, thinking of beer.

He enters a Danish café where men smoke long pipes and he planks his money down demanding drink. There is no one there to-night; no one he knows. He has another drink and goes on. (It is good to be back in dear old London!)

Out into Love Lane, across Cable Street, along Devonport Street into Commercial Road East. Here he meets the surge of London: the mellow lights that are to him London, the black-bearded men who are to him London; the sloe-eyed undulant maids who are to him London; the beckoning public-houses that are to him London! It does not seem strange to him that London should be an Oriental city. If you asked him for a symbol of London he would probably draw a picture of an ample young Jewess with Corinthian legs in sandy stockings.

Instinctively he calls at the corner 'pub' and puts down a pint of ale. He feels himself in the heart of London. He meets a friend who has just come in on a grain ship. He, too, is on the bosom of the metropolis. They stand each other drinks and talk shop, as all sailors do. It certainly has been an awful time at sea these last few weeks, but—it's good to be back in dear old London!

They go out into Commercial Road and think that it might be a brilliant and rather daring idea to walk towards Whitechapel. The lights beckon, the passing omnibuses give that thrill of life so remarkable after solitude; and the crowds of small, pert odalisques charm without, perhaps, arousing any deeper feeling as they move past, always two by two, an astonishing contrast to the wildness of the northern sea.

* * *

They decide to eat. They are in London! They are sick of the food given by cooks in flooded kitchens. They go into a restaurant where a faded patriarch in an apron offers them the menu. They eat Hungarian goulash followed by kugel, and they drink (becoming reckless and liking each other tremendously by now with the reckless friendliness of the blonde) a bottle of Alicante. Ah, how good to be in England, in London. . . .

They emerge and go on, following the omnibuses and the crowd, admiring the smouldering darkness of the girls, till they come to Aldgate, where various lines of traffic merge, where crowds merge, giving to Aldgate—or rather the northern side of it—an almost frantic excitement. It is the west end of the east! And here they pause. Few sailors—except those of America—ever travel beyond Aldgate Pump. Many have heard of the Nelson Column and of Piccadilly and Leicester Square and of Charing Cross, and many have identified these places beyond question at Aldgate!

This is the limit of London to the men who traffic on the seas. They do not know what lies beyond, and they do not want to know. Their bleak blue eyes are wide with the wonder of London: it certainly is a great city! What about another drink?

Like a couple of explorers on the edge of the unknown they enter that well-known bar where the dust is heavy and here they command beer.

'Cheerio!' they say in Scandinavian.

'Time, please!' says the chucker-out.

They put down their tankards and, drawing deep breaths, go out into the night. London is going home! The black-eyed beauties of London who parade at Aldgate are all walking the same way towards Whitechapel, the London restaurants with their Hebrew signboards are closing down, the London streets with their narrow alleyways are lying deserted in the light of pale lamps. . . .

The dock police scrutinize their tickets and they pass into the guarded darkness.

Good to be in London—the greatest city in the world!

A Suburban Dance

TAKE an omnibus or a tramcar in any direction and you will arrive in time at a suburban Piccadilly. Lights are shining. A queue waits outside a cinema, the public-houses are busy, the cheap restaurants are full, the streets are packed with aimless crowds, there is a whist drive in a hall, and a dance in another. There is a zest in the air which is absent from more expensive places. This night life ceases promptly at eleven-forty-five for its votaries have to be at work sharp at nine a.m. in the morning. It is the same at Brixton, Golders Green, Streatham, Cricklewood . . . little west ends of the suburbs complete with their own society, their own 'men about town', their own reigning beauties, their own heroes, villains, and enigmas. . . .

You give eighteenpence to a young woman who is imprisoned behind a brass grille, and you enter the dance hall.

The floor is covered with young men and girls fox-trotting to the music of an excellent band. The hall is large. Big yellow lanterns hang from the roof. Your first impression is that the girls are extraordinarily pretty and the men surprisingly ordinary. The girls have dressed for the dance; the men do not possess evening clothes. Here and there a star dancer has changed into a special kind of trousers, grey or black Oxford trousers as a rule, which billow over very pointed brown shoes. With these trousers he wears the coat and waistcoat of his lounge suit. Young men who do not dance linger in vague, drifting groups on the outskirts of the floor, smoking cigarettes and making comment. Pretty little wallflowers sit out by the dozen. Now and again two girls rise and dance together.

The music ends, the lights go up. Then a surprising thing occurs. In an instant men and girls have parted! The girls go over to one end of the room to sit on chairs ranged against the wall; the men group themselves in bands and coteries round the floor and light up the cigarettes which they had left parked on the radiator!

* * *

You look at the girls with interest. Most of them work in the big shops in the district. Each one wears a knee-short, tasteful evening frock and light stockings. You look along the rows of chairs and realize that here are seen the prettiest, neatest legs in London. In the Ritz, the Savoy, Claridge's, the pretty woman is easily picked out from the crowd; in this eighteenpenny suburban dance 'hop' a new beauty dawns on the sight each minute; the girls are all between the ages of sixteen and twenty-five. Perhaps that is the secret; they have abundant vitality and youth. They have also abundant lip-stick and powder, and one or two have Eton-cropped their heads.

It strikes you again and again that they are too vital and brilliant for the dull youths who lean against the wall and smoke cigarettes and whisper.

* * *

'Will you dance with me?' you ask.

She hesitates coyly, and looks as though she intends to cut you ice-cold.

'I don't mind if I do,' she replies, leaving a large leather handbag over the arm of her chair, and rising.

She glides in your arms like a spirit. She knows more about dancing than most people.

'Didn't those men look rather angry when I asked you to dance?' you say as you go round.

She shakes her hair in your face, looks up, and laughs.

'I should shay sho!'

'But why?'

'Well, you see, you don't know me, and you're a stranger.'

'Oh, I see. Then I've made a mistake?'

'I should shay sho,' she says brightly, and begins to hum in tune with the music.

The music ends.

'You dance beautifully. Will you dance with me again?'

'I must go to my friend. If I nod my head—yes; I'd like to.'

Off she goes quickly. All the other girls have dropped their men with equal speed. No man offers his partner a cup of coffee from the meagre buffet. Now and again girls two by two will grope in their leather handbags, discover sixpence, and pay for their own refreshment.

* * *

In all the smart hotels and dance places in London you will find that, generally speaking, the men are older than the women. In the suburban dance halls the men and the girls are contemporary. In the smart dance places of London the dance is the least important thing: in the dance hall it is the only thing that matters. Once it is over the girl has no use for her partner. She does not want to talk to him. She just shelves him and joins the pretty coloured bunch of *crêpe de Chine* against the wall. They sit whispering and smiling in a row like a collection of bright little humming birds on one long perch.

Is it imagination or is there a kind of suspicion between the male and the female?

There is no friendliness, no companionship, no dancers have apparently brought partners, each dance is the signal for the men to raid the humming birds, and the end of each dance is the signal for them to abandon them. You think that the bishops who fulminate against the immorality of the dance hall should put on ordinary clothes and go to one or two of them.

* * *

You go out where the omnibuses mass and the tramcars gather, realizing that they will all be at work again in the morning, feeling that you have blundered by chance into a club whose members were too well bred to object when you violated rules, marvelling at the high standard of beauty, wondering from how many dull homes Youth flies every night in a dance frock for a few hours of Bagdad, of music, of rhythm. . . .

As in the fairy tale, midnight ends the ball, and the Cinderellas of the suburbs put on velour coats and go home through dark streets.

'Pub Crawlers'

WHEN the public-houses open in the evening the pale old woman with the tray of collar studs and boot-laces begins her long and weary round. So does the man with one eye and many matches; so does the thin, consumptive-looking girl with a basket of flowers. They appeal to human nature in its most expansive moments.

When a normally hard-hearted man is emptying his fourth whisky down his red gullet he sees beneath his glass a pale alabaster hand, not too clean perhaps, grasping a box of matches or a string of boot-laces and, turning, he looks into eyes full of dumb misery. Something surprisingly soft inside him makes him hand out a few pennies with a gruff refusal to profit by the transaction:

'You can keep the studs,' he says.

Now and again the varied commercial travellers meet by chance under a lamp.

'Fourpence at the "Crown" and nothink at all at the "Nag"!'

'Go on! Ain't there anythink doing at the "Bunch o' Gripes"?'

'No; they said, "'Ullo, missus, you're the blinkin' fifth that's been in during the last five minutes!"'

It is a curious thing—but I have it on the authority of these people who live on saloon-bar generosity—that public-house philanthropy changes from night to night. On Monday the

'Nag's Head' may be full of kindness, and on Tuesday full of snubs; on Monday the 'White Horse' may rain pennies (and even sixpences), and on Tuesday you can put on your most wilted expression, and you won't get a blessed bean! So, you see, you have to keep on going round and round, night after night, taking the current of kindness as it comes.

You *have* to keep on, because there are children at home and a rent to be paid. . . .

Most remarkable of all the bar visitors is the Young Man with the Paper Shapes. Robert Louis Stevenson would have enjoyed him. He slips into a bar silently, and he stands by the door. Somehow the people become aware of him. Mrs. Jones, with her veil on her nose, pauses in mild alarm, with her second glass of stout poised above her ample bosom, as she says, *sotto voce*:

'Oo-er; look at 'im! What's he after?'

They see a pale young man gazing round the bar from beneath the brim of an old felt hat. He is fumbling with wads of folded newspaper contents bills, with which his clothes are padded. Quickly he makes little tearing movements, he pinches ovals and oblongs and stripes from the folded bill, he teases it and pulls it, and then opens it, displaying four perfectly modelled filigreed figures cut in the paper.

A delighted murmur rises from the bar! Isn't it clever? How does he do it? He ought to be on the halls!

* * *

Without a change of expression the young man brings out more folded bills, tears them, and exhibits this quick-change artistry to the bar. His *tour de force* is really remarkable (and it used to cost fourpence to perform before he bought old contents bills !) Taking a thick wad of bills from his pocket he makes a series of incisions with his fingers, he does something else difficult to follow, and then he opens out a paper ladder till it touches the ceiling. The higher the ceiling of the bar the more paper he uses ; so that he does not perform this trick till he feels more or less sure of his audience ! Then he sends round his hat, and you notice his well-shaped head. When he says, 'Thanks', you realize that he is not an unlettered man.

* * *

'I have been doing this, with the exception of the War, for about fifteen years,' he will tell you. 'You see, it's the only thing I can do. I learned how to do it from a man who, I believe, invented a turn like this on the halls. There is, I am told, another fellow doing this in London, but I have never seen him. . . . Like it ? One can't choose one's life ! Sometimes I do quite well. I collected eight shillings in one place the other night. They vary. One interested man in a bar and the whole bar forks out pennies and sixpences. . . .'

'Forgive my saying so, but you seem an unusual type to be living like this.'

'Unusual ? Perhaps I am ! The streets of London are full of unusual things. Did you know that a son of Sir —— plays a guitar in public-houses quite near here? I could show him to you to-night. When you have had to live on the streets in London nothing ever surprises you!'

'Are you married?'

'Oh, yes! I have two children, but my son is all right: he is at ——'

He mentions one of the best public schools in England! You feel that this young man is some relation to Stevenson's Young Man with the Cream Tarts! Who would imagine that a man taking pennies in bars could have a son at an expensive school which has raised several Prime Ministers and many of the greatest soldiers this country has known.

'Well, you see, my wife's people look after him!'

'And you look after—yourself?'

'I try to! Good night! I must be moving on! The most favourable moment at the "George" is just now, for the night engineering staff at X's take a half-hour's break! Good-night!'

He turns up his coat collar, turns down his hat brim over that pale, mysteriously refined face, and, with a shy nod to the goggle-eyed bar, dives out into the darkness.

A Night Club

HE is just back on six months' leave after years of policing the Libyan desert from the top of a camel. The girl he is going to marry is a dear, and she dances well. After we had seen her home, and he stood in the night with a brand new silk hat in his hand, listening to that terribly final click of a front door closing behind the beloved, he said to me :

'I don't feel like turning in. Shan't sleep a wink to-night. Surely London hasn't closed down ? '

I looked at his ingenuous brick-red face and knew that he was about to ask me to take him to a night club. Like all visitors and colonials who visit this city he wanted to look upon life in the rough, he wanted to sit thrilled and horrified on the apex of his superiority and observe men and women—particularly women—dance along the primrose path to the everlasting bonfire. A kind of mental liqueur after a good evening.

I looked at his blue eyes and that healthy schoolboy enthusiasm in them, marvelling that a man who is a terror to the thieving nomad when he swoops up out of the sand at the head of his patrol, cross-legged on a camel, should need any thrill in life ! It occurred to me that I might as well cure him.

'The Hell Fire Club ? ' he said. 'Jove, we're going it a bit, aren't we ? '

The taxicab turned and went back towards Piccadilly.

* * *

When we entered, three tired waiters were leaning against an aggressive yellow wall as if they were presiding over the funeral bakemeats. One yawned, and the others caught it. An anaemic young man, who is apparently never awake when the barbers are, played a piano with an expression he will wear later in Hades, a trap drummer crouched over his instruments with half-shut eyes ; but no one danced.

We sat in an alcove and ordered ham and eggs. All round the tiny room, sitting in similar alcoves, were men and women drenched in gloom. The women looked frayed, the men looked bored. They seemed as though they were attending a wake in evening dress. You wondered where the body was.

'Is this a blind, or are they really like this ?' asked the Man from the Desert.

'No ; this is their usual state of mind. It's the same every night.'

'Then why don't they go home ?'

'They can't ; it's one of the mysteries of London.'

As we ate our ham and eggs we looked round sympathetically. The only virtue of the place was its complete honesty ; no one was pretending to enjoy it. You know, after a dinner-party, how you sit round discussing people, forgetting the clock, and then comes a time when discussion peters out and you still sit on under a spell thinking that there is something else to say: and there is not. You drift on in a kind of tired stupor which it is difficult to break. It requires real effort to say: 'Well, what about bed?'

'Of course, it's attractive in a way,' said the Man from the Desert. 'As an American would say, it "keeps you guessing".'

'Yes, but there's nothing to guess. . . .

'I feel that all these people are waiting for something dreadful to happen.'

'Well, you're wrong. It happened when they joined the club.'

* * *

Some excitement was caused, but not shown, when a man and a girl danced. Everybody watched for at least two minutes, and the trap drummer opened his eyes.

A man at the next table called over the waiter, and with a heavy air of decision, as if he were about to order a revolver and end his misery, said, 'Two black coffees.'

'Did you hear?' whispered the Man from the Desert. 'He's ordered two black coffins!'

The waiter moved off as if he was thoroughly competent to find them!

* * *

'Jove!' cried the desert patrol suddenly, 'what a stunning girl! And she's alone. I wonder who she is? . . .'

'That would be difficult to say. I can tell you what she is: she is a dance instructress, one of the new professions. She has a good eye for clothes. Like a blonde barmaid she attracts custom. It you would like to dance with her you can. Afterwards you will carelessly leave a pound note on the table. You understand?'

'But she's a lady!' whispered the desert patrol.

'We'll see,' I replied, calling the head waiter.

* * *

The girl smiled and moved across to us.

'Good evening,' she said.

'Do have a drink,' said the desert patrol.

'I'd adore some champagne,' replied the girl.

She was beautifully dressed. Her clothes were good and she wore them as only a woman can who has always worn good clothes. The desert patrol was right: she was a lady. The conversation skimmed a foolish surface. I caught the desert patrol looking at her in a way that told me that his mind was full of the problem: why had she 'come down' to this; what explanation lay behind her appearance in a fuggy, unhealthy little night club.

'Well, fancy you knowing the Vyners,' cried the desert patrol. 'Old Dick was killed in Egypt. I knew him well. I say, forgive me, do you come from that part of the world?'

The girl sipped her champagne and looked at

the inoffensive face over the glass, seeming to hesitate.

'As a matter of fact,' she replied, 'I do, or rather I did. Let's dance. . . .'

They danced; and I admired them. She was a beautiful girl. She might have been his sister. When the dance was over they settled at her table and began talking. They danced again. The desert patrol looked worried. They settled again. A swarthy young man with incipient side-whiskers cut into their conversation and the desert patrol, rising, excused himself and came back to me, looking rather pink about the ears:

'Let's go!' he said. 'I've had enough of this place. London's a pretty foul spot, old boy. . . . Oh, nothing, I'll tell you when we get outside. . . .'

We found our hats and walked out into the cool night air. A slow taxicab cruised along the kerb as we walked towards Piccadilly. A policeman with a lamp on his belt tried shop doors; a vague figure moved out of the lamplight as we approached and half said something . . . chill, desolate Piccadilly. . . .

'What's the trouble?' I asked him.

'Who the devil do you think that girl is? She's the daughter of old Colonel X, a pal of my guv'nors. I've heard about her. I believe my sister knows her. They have a big old place down in ———. She was a quiet, inoffensive kid till about a year ago, when she suddenly went crazy and left home. My sister wrote to me about it at the time, but I'd forgotten till I heard her name.

And this is what she's doing, touting round these filthy night clubs. . . .'

'Did you attempt to reform her?'

'Well, I . . . anyhow she told me politely to keep my mouth shut and mind my own business. She isn't a bit repentant. Just fancy a girl brought up in the country with plenty of money and all that . . . and she seems happy! That's perhaps the queerest thing! I could understand it if she was too proud to go home; but she's too contented with this vile dancing life of hers to go home. How do you explain it?'

'The most unexpected people "go bad". It's a tragic thing. That's where you find them now and again, in night clubs. There is something about the mad atmosphere that seems to act on them like a drug.'

'Can nothing be done about it?'

'Nothing. The first stage is that and the next is drugs. For the final stage you watch the evening papers.'

'But it's criminal to let a girl like that slide away into the bad.'

'What can you do? She's over age. She's her own mistress. She can only be cured by herself.'

I told the desert patrol some of the queer people who have sunk themselves in the squalor of the London night.

'Well,' he said, 'you can keep London.'

To Anywhere

STRANGE things happen now and then if you just take the first omnibus and sit there long enough.

It may have been a 2b or a 116 or an 11 or a 3—I don't know—but I sat there in the back corner seat with four-pennyworth of possibility stuck in the strap of my wrist watch, and was carried swiftly on the level of first floor windows through the varied scent of a warm London evening. (Some people eat fried fish all the year round.)

There were long grim streets, horrible as streets but thrilling as collections of little homes, each one in its way unique; and there were long holds-up at congested junctions where tramcars and omnibuses tied themselves into knots and bunched together like a silly flock of sheep till a policeman walked to one side; and then they untied again.

* * *

When you are tired, or when you consciously turn off your brain as a tap is turned off, you can float along in a delicious haze, hardly existing, feeling that it is rather funny that you should be you, faintly amused or placidly interested in the life round you, much as a sleepy man in a cinema follows the pictures, grasping nothing of their significance or continuity; just conscious that things are flickering and fluttering in front of his eyes. I was conscious that the man and the girl in front of me were holding hands, and I thought how lucky for them that they had managed to coincide in time. A little matter of twenty years between them—a nothing to time—and where would they be now? Life is full of these hair-breadth escapes.

* * *

It was that time when London, its day's work done, does not quite know what to do with itself till bedtime. Men leant from windows in shirt sleeves reading the evening papers, women talked and shopped; young girls who had hurriedly changed their work clothes were two by two tripping along in their best clothes, setting out on that nightly parade which for lack of social occasions is the only way they have of meeting young men of their own age. All exceedingly proper and conventional.

'Oh, he looks such a nice boy! Shall we turn round, Maudie?'

They turn as two sheepish lads approach and raise their hats.

'Didn't we meet you at the pictures last week?' say the boys foolishly, putting up a barrage of pretence, knowing that they did not and knowing that the girls know they know it.

'No, you didn't,' say the girls with that swift feminine intuition if they feel the boys are 'wrong uns', or 'P'raps you did', and giggle.

This means that one of the boys may say:

'What about a walk?' and after pretending that mother would be annoyed, and saying: 'Oh, I don't know. What do you think, Maudie?' they giggle and remark: 'Well, we don't mind if we do.'

Not an elegant way of meeting your fellow creatures, but what can they do? I suppose thousands of happy marriages started like this.

* * *

Suddenly I was startled out of this triviality by something that looked remarkable. While I was still in a coma, and regarding it freshly as if I had never seen it before, it appealed to me as one of those hallucinations which bothered Don Quixote from time to time. I got off the omnibus quickly.

Here was an enormous green space stretching into the evening mists. Everything that can happen on a green space was happening simultaneously on this one. Bare-legged children were paddling in a pond on the edge of the green. Men and boys were playing cricket. There was tennis. Hundreds of people lay on the grass. Placid old women sat up stiffly knitting under trees. A young man lay luxuriously with his head in a girl's lap. There were dogs barking, and, somewhere, a band.

It looked as horrible as Utopia, a place where humanity had suddenly decided to do as it liked and blow the consequences. I plunged into it. A cricket ball whizzed over my head. I passed through segments of varied enthusiasm, now mixed up with tennis players, now in the middle of a political meeting, now daringly walking across a juvenile Lord's, now watching a serious grown-up game of cricket, now stepping over an occasional unconscious body stretched on the grass in an attitude of death.

But the most remarkable sight was an enclosure containing a hearty band in which over bumpy turf girls were dancing with one another while young men looked on sniggering and longing to have enough courage to join in. Occasionally one did; and the others laughed at him. This was a kind of cheap edition of Merrie England with the joy gone; the impetus that led people to dance for the sheer love of life absent.

Slowly the moon rose and gained strength. The enthusiasts left Utopia. Lovers drifted slowly under the moon. A boy asked me for a cigarette card. There was no sound but the clang of a tramcar bell. I felt in the cool emptiness of this towny grass that people had been very happy and I determined some day to go back and find out why.

'Where am I?' I asked a policeman.

He looked at me suspiciously and replied:

'Peckham Rye.'

Our Last Inn

Written at the George Inn, Southwark,
September, 1926

WITHIN a hundred yards of London Bridge I am going to bed by candle-light. The last office of the chambermaid was to carry into this queer old room a big enamelled hip-bath with the question: 'Hot or cold in the morning, sir?' A canopied four-poster bed occupies a large portion of the room. It is a high state couch of great splendour. It looks as though it should be mounted on wheels so that it could be drawn through the streets with a sultana lying inside on silk cushions. Or it looks, with the white sheets turned back, as if ready for the lying-in-state of a French President. That is possibly far-fetched: most of all it looks as though against its generous pillows should recline an eighteenth-century belle with a lace cap on her Greuze-like head. She would, of course, be sipping chocolate.

Placed against the side from which, I suppose, I am to enter this imposing bed is a mounting-block of three little steps covered in carpet. How often in hotels all over the world have I speculated idly on the past occupants of my room, a reflection frequently assisted by a subtle perfume left behind in a wardrobe or a forlorn hairpin in a drawer; but here in this forgotten old inn, the last inn in Southwark, a man can actually see the steps by which men and women long gathered to a sounder sleep have mounted to their dreams. The candle-light casts shadows: it flings a caricature of the four posts slantwise against the farther wall, and although it is a warm September night I feel chilled by the thought that if I looked up suddenly from this paper I *might* see shining on the bed-steps the ghost of a small naked foot.

Some rooms watch a man as a suspicious animal, unable to make up its mind about him. This room is like that. I write without fear of contradiction that it is the most remarkable bedroom in London. There is something about it—a something common to many ancient rooms—that makes me anxious to placate it and to find favour with its shadows. . . . The fitful traffic of the Borough High Street goes by outside at the end of the 'yard', just shaking the window-frame slightly. Downstairs in the dark inn a clock strikes eleven.

I have for years promised myself that I would some day find time to spend a night here; and I have been postponing the pleasure as one does, now and then, postpone pleasure. The George Inn, the last of the famous coaching inns of Southwark, suffered in all the Borough fires, and although the site is that of the St. George Inn mentioned in 1554 as situated on the north side of the Tabard, the present building dates from the eighteenth century. Praise to those men who two hundred years ago rebuilt the 'George' on the medieval plan: it is the only galleried inn in London. If I opened the bedroom door and crossed the adjacent sitting-room I would find myself on an oak gallery like the deck of a galleon. Here it was in the old days that men leaned, watching the coach swing in under the archway, commenting on the new arrivals and the condition of the horses. Miss Murray, who has kept the George Inn for the last fifty years remembers when the gallery was complete. Some time ago when Guy's Hospital, who owned the land, sold it to the Great Northern Railway Company two sides of the old building with their galleries were demolished to make way for a goods depot. The side mercifully preserved is one of the unique treasures of London.

It seems to me that the shadows are like fingers pointing; that this old room is trying to say to me: 'The time may come when you, and those who love London, may have to fight for all that is left of me!' and the knowledge that I would indeed fight hard places me in sympathy with the shadows, which no longer appear to watch doubtfully.

I have made friends with this queer old room.

* * *

I must go to bed; but I am not tired and I wish to postpone the climb. . . .

I shall never forget my arrival here this evening. I hate arriving at a modern hotel to be shot up in a lift to a stereotyped room in which to the servants I become 'Number 209'. I have inherited from who knows how many coaching ancestors a keen perception of the technique of arriving at an inn. It is something that this age has lost. Even a millionaire taking possession of the best suite in Claridge's cannot achieve the faintest ghost of the pleasure of arriving unexpectedly and importantly at an inn which, recognizing you as 'the quality', flings itself into quick activity to give you the best it has. In my own life this has happened only twice—once in Somerset and once at Lillebonne, in France. There is a subtle flattery in the sudden bustle that follows your arrival; a delicious deference in the voice of the landlord as he flings open the door of his best room and hopes 'it will do'; the smell and sizzle of a roasting chicken; the bent back of the chambermaid kindling a fire; the steps of the landlord ascending with a bottle of his best wine, all give you the feeling, impossible in the Ritz, that people are not only serving you well but that they are also glad to do so.

Something of the kindness of the old inn welcome lingers on at the 'George'. People rarely stay here now. Few people realize that it is possible to sleep in London's last coaching inn.

Miss Murray was sitting reading in the little bar parlour, which is typical of all Old English inn parlours of the eighteenth century. Above the bottles and the decanters hung two horse-pistols discovered years ago in an oak chest. They were used by the coach guards. With them was found a pouch full of shot as big as marbles.

'Can I stay here?' I asked.

'Certainly,' smiled Miss Murray.

I learned afterwards how sincerely she loves this

old inn of hers, so that I am now able to translate her smile into words. It meant:

'For five hundred years travellers have been staying at the "George" and the "George" is not dead yet! Of course you can stay.'

Then she showed me this room with its great four-poster and I knew that here at least Time has not been able to pick the door lock. As I unpacked I heard orders given about dinner; for the coffee-room was shrouded.

I am the only guest in the 'George'.

* * *

After dinner, served in the 'coffee-room' where the tables are placed between high-backed settles, I went into the bar parlour to drink port. I would rather have ordered whisky, but that, I felt, would have insulted the ghosts.

'Once,' said Miss Murray, 'we were busy with the hop merchants from the Hop Exchange near here. They used to come up from Kent and spend the night. But now they come up by motor and return the same evening. We do not have many visitors now. We do a luncheon trade, but no dinners.'

Years ago Miss Murray knew a man who said that he had many a time met and chatted to Charles Dickens in the coffee-room of the 'George':

'He brings it into *Little Dorrit*,' said Miss Murray, 'as the room where Tip Dorrit went to write a letter.'

The writing-table is still in the coffee-room, with pen, ink, and paper!

I do not know a spot in London which is more truly Dickens London than the bar and the coffee-room of this inn. The 'Cheshire Cheese' in Fleet Street has survived change, but in the process it has become terribly self-conscious: the old 'George' is supremely unself-conscious. It caters not for the American sightseer but for the traveller and for the merchants of Southwark, for whom it has always catered. They have eaten its mutton for centuries. This inn has not been preserved: it is a genuine survival. There is life in the old 'George' still!

I sat drinking port in the room which Mr. E. V. Lucas so aptly describes in his *London Revisited* as 'a paradise of bottles', wondering how long ago it is since the last coach clattered into the yard.

'I have no idea of the date,' said Miss Murray, 'but once, many years ago, an old gentleman came here and asked for a room. When I told him that I could put him up for the night he said, "And it isn't the first time either! The last time I stayed here I came on the coach!" So, of course, I gave him the best bedroom. He was over eighty years old. Ah, times have changed . . . all London has changed. . . .'

'Except the old "George".'

'Well, I've tried to keep it as I always remember it.'

At the side of the bar parlour is a glass window which opens on to a passage. I became aware of a dark, spectral man standing outside tapping on the window with his finger nail. The window was opened and the light shone on him.

'Half a pint, miss!' he said.

He jumped me! He looked exactly like Mr. Jingle. . . .

The candle has burned to the last two inches and it is nearly midnight. I cannot say that the mighty bed invites me: it could never be so familiar. It looms before me like a state coach. Now the traffic is stilled. I would dearly like to go out to the balcony and look down at the ghosts of the inn yard, but the floors creak and I might awaken the 'George'. The strangest thing about to-night is that I am in London in 1926!

Continued in the morning.

I am at the best of times an indifferent sleeper. I mounted the three steps and climbed into the great bed; and felt marvellously awake. I heard a clock strike twelve.

I began to think of the Tabard, which stood nearby, and of Chaucer. I enjoyed the feeling that I was lying so near to London Bridge. I wondered if Shakespeare had ever stayed at the 'George'. He must have known of it; possibly he dined here on occasions . . . the silence of London. In the West End the wheels go round to the small hours, but in Southwark there is silence at midnight. The 'George' creaks now and then. Strange, furtive creaks. . . . It is a curious sensation to slip out of your period into another age. This bed was a genuine escape from modern London; this room was insulated from the London we know: it seemed to me in that hazy condition between sleep and wakefulness that I might at any moment hear the voice of the night watchman and see the light of his lantern move across the ceiling.

'Twelve o'clock on a fine night. All's well!'

He would say something like that. . . . Surely the ghost of the Dover Coach glides into the yard below on dark nights! If ghosts were a little more convincing how much more interesting life would be. I suppose many a fair refugee lay in this bed during the French Revolution, dreaming of the sound of tumbrils on the cobblestones of the Rue St. Honoré. Many a fair refugee . . . many a fair refugee . . . and how many times have runaway couples sought refuge here on their way to London?

'The "George" is no place for ladies,' said Miss Murray to me after dinner, 'if they want a lot of fussing. It's all right if you take us as you find us and don't ask for the bathroom, because we haven't got one and don't miss it and manage to have baths just the same!'

I suppose runaway ladies didn't want a lot of fussing. . . . It must have been exciting to elope with a girl in a coach, to hold her hand and say brave things as you swayed over rough roads, hoping against hope that none of the horses would cast a shoe, looking out of the windows at the pale light left over from the sunset, seeing the rain in the wheel ruts of the road. It must have been exciting! Then you would come at length to some little galleried inn at night with a yellow lamp shining among Virginia creeper in the gallery, and the horses would be blowing and stamping on the cobbles as you hammered at the door and asked for the best room and lights, dinner and a bottle of wine. For her ladyship and yourself . . . her ladyship . . .

And as the coachman let down the little hanging steps you would hand her out delicately. Hand in hand you would go up to the room and light every candle in every sconce and hold her hands and look at her. Just as you were about to kiss her for minutes on end a sleepy varlet with a bit of straw in his hair would blunder in with an apron full of wood logs for the fire. You would go over to the window in an offhand way and pull the curtain aside, watching them take the coach through to the stables.

'My soul . . .' you would begin as the inn-keeper entered with a cold shoulder of mutton.

Your man would tell you when he brought up the luggage that the Dover Coach was next yours in the stable. That would alarm you, and her ladyship's eyes would grow wide as the most beautiful saucers.

'My good fellow,' you would say to the inn-keeper, 'did any gentlemen come over from France on the packet to-night?'

'Only one, me lord—in the next room, me lord.'

'And his name?'

'Sir Timothy Dagger, me lord.'

Merciful heavens, her husband. . . . Yes; it must have been exciting and complicated and—confound this bed!—probably not worth it in the long run when you met on wet grass in a mushroom mist, wondering which of you would be the man to finish his breakfast properly . . . .

At this point, I suppose, I fell asleep

* * *

There came a knock on the door. The chambermaid entered and began to fill the hip-bath:

'A fine morning, sir,' she said.

Four huge jugs full of water went into the hip bath and left enough water to splash in. I could not resist the temptation before I shaved of wandering out on the inn balcony and looking down towards the railway goods depot! What a revenge the railway has taken! I leaned on the gallery and looked at the ugly blank wall opposite and wished with all my heart that I could rebuild the lost portions of the 'George' and give London a coaching inn to be a joy and an escape.

Before breakfast I took a walk across London Bridge and watched the tangle of carts jammed round Billingsgate. I realized as I took this short walk that I had really spent a night in London.

(Another remarkable discovery is that the chambermaid, through sheer womanly kindness of heart, has darned two pairs of my socks!)

Dawn over London

THE vitality of Piccadilly ebbs after midnight hour by hour till three a.m., at which time a human figure becomes enigmatic in the emptiness of the Circus. At no time is the absence of the light-footed deity of Victorian London so noticeable: the hoardings in the centre of the roadway are like a scar.

Piccadilly at three a.m. has the dead appearance of an empty stage in an empty theatre. The mind, associating it with moving life and the excitement of great crowds, finds it uncanny: an abnormal sight, so cold and bare under the watchful yellow lights, so ready, it seems, for the bizarre. This is the time when policemen do not even smile as a man wearing a false nose slows up his motor-car in the Circus to inquire the nearest way to an obscure crescent in Maida Vale. At three a.m. Piccadilly would be an ideal stage for a performance of the Russian Ballet. All the comic and grotesque in life should come up like a toadstool at this time, in this place. . . .

* * *

'You wouldn't hardly think Piccadilly could be so quiet, would you?' said the policeman.

'I suppose things happen now and then?'

'Not often. A drunk! A suspicious character

loitering with intent! You have to keep your eyes open.'

He laughed.

'See that bin over there where they keep the grit for the road? One night I saw the lid move! I thought I'd "got 'em," but I looked again and sure enough—it moved! It was just about the time when we were on the watch for a crook suspected of a big West End jewel robbery. "Now that's funny!" I thought, so I went over quietly and waited. The lid came up and banged down again, then it opened wide, and up sat a young fellow, just like a jack-in-the-box. "What are you doing in there?" I said. "I don't know where I am," he replied. "Do you know this bin is the property of the Westminster Council," I said, "and I could arrest you for trespassing?" I could see he was all right and I was only pulling his leg. . . .

'He was in a blinkin' awful mess! He was a young gent right enough—in evening dress—and he had grit in his hair and in his collar and his waistcoat pockets. "Help me out of this!" he said. "Not till you give an account of yourself," I said. "Who are you?" He scratched some more grit out of his head and said, "I'm the best man!" "Well," I said, "you're the worst-looking man I've seen in the Circus for many a long time, and that's a fact." . . . To cut a long story short, it appeared that he'd been to a bachelor party, and his pals had put him in the bin for a lark. He must have been awful drunk, for he fell asleep. The job we had with his hat! He'd been sleeping on it!

Anyhow, we punched it out. . . . Good night, sir!'

* * *

Leicester Square was empty save for a stray figure loitering like a ghost.

'Open all night.'

Here is the sequel to the desolation of Piccadilly! In the all-night cafés—in an atmosphere of stale smoke and hot coffee—is drawn all the life of the streets. The place is crowded with men and women sitting on little gold wicker chairs at close-packed tables. The room is full all night long. The air is loud all night long with the talk of these night birds. There is a curious refugee atmosphere. Most of the men wear their overcoats. The primitive magnet of warmth, light, and food has drawn them in from the cold and the dark. Meeting this unsuspected vitality in the night is rather like boarding a liner in the desolation of mid-ocean and finding yourself in a great restaurant. Just as in a liner you are conscious that the ocean is beyond the windows, so in these places the darkness of Piccadilly seems very close, in spite of the bright light, the chatter, the waiters with their steaming trays. . . .

* * *

Who are these people? The eye that delights in crowds moves over them with interest, for this is the most varied crowd in London's twenty-four hours. There are young girls who have given up walking about outside. They sit together at tables intent in conversation. There is a free-masonry between them and a uniform type of young man—pugilistic young men, or pale, tight-waisted young men with sallow faces, the type that tries to sell postcards under the Arc de Triomphe.

Mixed with them in the craziest fashion are smart people who have been having a night out . . . boys whose white shirt fronts shine obtrusively ; young girls in evening cloaks who lean bare arms on the table and smoke cigarettes reflectively as they regard the obvious characters present with a cool interest which their grandmothers would have considered revolting. Silk hats appear. Ham and eggs quick ! A bunch of tough-looking fellows come in, their coat-collars turned up, their eyes searching the crowd beneath caps and the brims of hats. They discover their associates, and move over to them, settle down and whisper. It looks suspicious ! You watch them, half expecting to see Lady Flash's diamonds pass from hand to hand !

Are they the London apache ? Are they a third-class dance band off duty ?

There are more dramatic possibilities here than in the entire East End of London, that libelled district which (mostly) goes to bed at ten !

* * *

A young man enters. A girl sits up and her eyes take fire :

'There he is, the dirty cad !'

Her three friends hold her down.

'Let me tell him what I think of him!'

'Hush! Don't be a fool, Maudie! Shut up!'

Somehow the flash of fire dies. A queer atmosphere! The girls from Knightsbridge and Kensington gaze through their cigarette smoke, mildly thrilled. Something ugly might at any moment bubble up in this varied haphazard crowd which is sheltering from the darkness. That is the feeling. . . .

* * *

Outside, a derelict, an old shuffling man who has now given up begging, stands beneath a lamp and carefully opens a dirty newspaper in which is some horrid fragment picked from a restaurant refuse bin.

At the corner, where there is a pillar-box, a pretty girl who has been running hard, posts a letter. Another girl, also running, cries:

'Oh, you little fool—now you've done it! And you deserve what's coming to you!'

Yet Piccadilly seems so dead under the watchful lamps. Over the rest of London is the peace of sleep. . . .

The London night is ending. . . .

It is not yet dawn and it is not night; it is that short between-time when the fates seem gathered in prayer over London. Already work has begun. Over the bridges pass the tramcars; from Covent Garden rises a rumble of effort; but it is still dark. The streets are empty; Big Ben's four gold faces shine to the four points of the compass; the Thames runs on in darkness under the lit bridges. It is very cold. . . .

I have seen dawn in many places; in Jerusalem I have seen light come fretfully like a thin sword above the mountains; a streak that widens and cuts a way out of the darkness for the shell-pink galleons to sail up from the east as they flush the minarets; I have seen the sun go up above the Sahara like a gong that calls the world to life; and I have seen the Egyptian sun leap in one second round and hot above the red Arabian hills. But dawn comes to London slowly.

A little wind slips out of the east and blows through the lamplit streets. Gradually the lamplight loses its brilliance and a kind of greyness in which stars fade one by one comes over all things. The black shadows which have wrapped London during the night pale moment by moment.

The Thames becomes a grey river like a streak of blown smoke, and, slowly, the light touches first the dome of St. Paul's, then the high steeples of Wren's white churches. You stand thinking that London at this moment looks like a harbour full of ships whose white masts lie against the sky. You become aware of a shrillness in the air. The London sparrows! Second by second the grey light strengthens. You see a great flight of small birds go north; the starlings that nest in London and fly with the dawn to the fields.

* * *

Dawn over London

It is marvellous to stand alone leaning over the parapet of the bridge, watching the curve of the Embankment grow clear like the image on a photographic plate coming up in a dark room ; and you are lost in the wonder of dawn and in the drama of dawn over a great city.

For now London's millions are coming out of dreams into reality. In thousands of homes the shrill clamour of the alarm clock is calling to duty, and, through the curtains, men and women see a thin streak of grey. And you know that this dawn means for some happiness, for some sorrow ; you know that among that dark mystery of roofs and chimneys are some who welcome the light and some who fear it ; some who awaken with a smile ; some who awaken with a brain drugged by sleep for one merciful second before the weight of a misery reasserts itself.

Every city on earth appears to have washed out its sins in the night. Dawn comes to them with eternal beauty and freshness. They seem to be making a fresh start every day. Through their streets, empty of men and women, is something which says :

'Here is a new day ! See how clean and clear it is over your stones, as fresh and pure as the light that comes over hills and fields.'

London in the dawn is a clean, unwritten page.

You lean over the bridge and know that in a few hours the streets will be full of noise and people ; the sensations of the evening papers are yet unborn. There may be a murder, a suicide . . . and you feel that in some way all the things which people will be discussing in the next dusk are now locked up in this calm greyness. It should seem an ominous greyness, but it does not. It is a pure, beautiful thing like snow before men tread it into mud.

* * *

It is now light.

In the east there comes a pink flush low in the sky. The sun has risen. It is a smouldering short-lived pinkness as if the sun were fighting hard to show himself, uncertain, troubled. The colour changes, the pink clouds fade into the grey. The cross above St. Paul's is gold. The street lights go out. The feeling of other-worldliness has vanished with the dawn light, which went suddenly as if London had flung off a wrap. Now all is clear to the eyes. Over the bridges sounds the rumble of wheels. London, the most masculine city in the world, seems standing clean and stripped, like a boxer entering a ring, for another twenty-four rounds with Fate.

NOTE

With the exception of ' Our Last Inn ', which has not appeared elsewhere, these glimpses of London after dark were first published in the columns of the *Daily Express*.

H. V. M.

LONDON
October 1926

Printed by Jarrold & Sons, Ltd., Norwich

METHUEN'S GENERAL LITERATURE

A SELECTION OF

MESSRS. METHUEN'S PUBLICATIONS

This Catalogue contains only a selection of the more important books published by Messrs. Methuen. A complete catalogue of their publications may be obtained on application.

ANSTEY (F.).
THE YOUNG RECITER AND MODEL MUSIC-HALL. 5*s.* net.

ARMSTRONG (Anthony).
YESTERDAILIES. Illustrated. 5*s.* net.
LIVESTOCK IN BARRACKS. Illustrated by E. H. SHEPARD. 6*s.* net.
WARRIORS AT EASE.
WARRIORS STILL AT EASE.
PERCIVAL AND I.
PERCIVAL AT PLAY.
HOW TO DO IT.
ME AND FRANCES.
APPLE AND PERCIVAL.
SELECTED WARRIORS.
Each 3*s.* 6*d.* net.

BAIN (F. W.).
IN THE GREAT GOD'S HAIR.
A DRAUGHT OF THE BLUE.
AN INCARNATION OF THE SNOW.
A MINE OF FAULTS.
A DIGIT OF THE MOON.
THE LIVERY OF EVE.
A HEIFER OF THE DAWN.
AN ESSENCE OF THE DUSK.
THE DESCENT OF THE SUN.
THE ASHES OF A GOD.
BUBBLES OF THE FOAM.
A SYRUP OF THE BEES.
THE SUBSTANCE OF A DREAM.
Each 3*s.* 6*d.* net.

BELLOC (H.).
A HISTORY OF ENGLAND. In Seven Volumes. Vols. I, II, III and IV. Each 15*s.* net.
MARIE ANTOINETTE. Illustrated. 18*s.* net.
PARIS. Illustrated. 8*s.* 6*d.* net.
THE PYRENEES. Illustrated. 8*s.* 6*d.* net.
ON NOTHING.
HILLS AND THE SEA.
ON SOMETHING.
FIRST AND LAST.
ON.
THIS AND THAT.
ON ANYTHING.
ON EVERYTHING.
EMMANUAL BURDEN.
A PICKED COMPANY.
Each 3*s.* 6*d.* net.

BIRMINGHAM (George A.).
A WAYFARER IN HUNGARY. Illustrated. 8*s.* 6*d.* net.
SPILLIKINS.
SHIPS AND SEALING-WAX.
Two Volumes of Essays. Each 3*s.* 6*d.* net.

CARR (Philip).
THE FRENCH AT HOME. Illustrated. 10*s.* 6*d.* net.
DAYS WITH THE FRENCH ROMANTICS IN THE PARIS OF 1830. Illustrated. 15*s.* net.

CHESTERTON (G. K.).
ALL IS GRIST. 6s. net.
G. K. C. AS M.C. Edited by J. P. DE FONSEKA. 7s. 6d. net.
GENERALLY SPEAKING.
THE OUTLINE OF SANITY.
TREMENDOUS TRIFLES.
A MISCELLANY OF MEN.
ALARMS AND DISCURSIONS.
COME TO THINK OF IT . . .
CHARLES DICKENS.
ALL THINGS CONSIDERED.
FANCIES VERSUS FADS.
THE FLYING INN.
THE USES OF DIVERSITY.
THE BALLAD OF THE WHITE HORSE
Each 3s. 6d. net.
WINE, WATER AND SONG. 1s. 6d. net.

CURLE (J. H.).
THIS WORLD FIRST. TO-DAY AND TO-MORROW.
Each 6s. net.
THIS WORLD OF OURS. 7s. 6d. net.
THE SHADOW-SHOW. 6s. net. and 3s. 6d. net.

EINSTEIN (Albert).
RELATIVITY: THE SPECIAL AND GENERAL THEORY. 5s. net.
SIDELIGHTS ON RELATIVITY. 3s. 6d. net.
THE MEANING OF RELATIVITY. 5s. net.
THE BROWNIAN MOVEMENT. 5s. net.

EISLER (Robert).
THE MESSIAH JESUS AND JOHN THE BAPTIST. Illustrated. £2 2s. net.

FINER (Herman).
THE THEORY AND PRACTICE OF MODERN GOVERNMENT. Two Volumes £2 2s. net.

FYLEMAN (Rose).
FAIRIES AND CHIMNEYS. THE FAIRY GREEN.
THE FAIRY FLUTE.
Each 2s. net.
FAIRIES AND FRIENDS.
FORTY GOOD-NIGHT TALES.
FORTY GOOD-MORNING TALES.
THE RAINBOW CAT.
THE ADVENTURE CLUB.
TWENTY TEA-TIME TALES.
EIGHT LITTLE PLAYS FOR CHILDREN.
SEVEN LITTLE PLAYS FOR CHILDREN.
Each 3s. 6d. net.
A GARLAND OF ROSES: Collected Poems. Illustrated. 5s. net.
A PRINCESS COMES TO OUR TOWN. Illustrated. 5s. net.
THE STRANGE ADVENTURES OF CAPTAIN MARWHOPPLE. Illustrated. 3s. 6d. net.
FIFTY-ONE NEW NURSERY RHYMES. Illustrated in Colour. 6s. net.

GIBBON (Edward).
THE DECLINE AND FALL OF THE ROMAN EMPIRE. Edited, with Notes, Appendixes, and Maps, by J. B. BURY. Illustrated. Seven Volumes. Each 15s. net. Also, unillustrated. Seven Volumes. Each 7s. 6d. net.

GLOVER (T. R.).
THE CONFLICT OF RELIGIONS IN THE EARLY ROMAN EMPIRE. 10s. 6d. net.
POETS AND PURITANS. 10s. 6d. net.
VIRGIL. 10s. 6d. net.
FROM PERICLES TO PHILIP. 12s. 6d. net.

GRAHAME (Kenneth).
THE WIND IN THE WILLOWS. 7s. 6d. net. Also Pocket Edition, 3s. 6d. net. Leather, 7s. 6d. net. Also illustrated by ERNEST H. SHEPARD. 7s. 6d. net. *See also* **Milne (A. A.).**

HADFIELD (J. A.).
PSYCHOLOGY AND MORALS. 6s. net.

HALL (H. R.).

THE ANCIENT HISTORY OF THE NEAR EAST. Illustrated. £1 1*s*. net.
THE CIVILIZATION OF GREECE IN THE BRONZE AGE. Illustrated. £1 10*s*. net.

HEATON (Rose Henniker).

THE PERFECT HOSTESS. Decorated by ALFRED E. TAYLOR. 7*s*. 6*d*. net. Also wedding present or gift edition, £1 1*s*. net.
THE PERFECT SCHOOLGIRL. 3*s*. 6*d*. net.

HERBERT (A. P.).

HELEN. 2*s*. 6*d*. net.
DERBY DAY. 2*s*. 6*d*. net.
TANTIVY TOWERS. 2*s*. 6*d*. net.
WISDOM FOR THE WISE. 5*s*. net.
HONEYBUBBLE & CO. 3*s*. 6*d*. net.
MISLEADING CASES IN THE COMMON LAW. 5*s*. net.
MORE MISLEADING CASES. 5*s*. net.
THE BOMBER GIPSY. 3*s*. 6*d*. net.
THE WHEREFORE AND THE WHY. Illustrated. 3*s*. 6*d*. net.
THE SECRET BATTLE. 3*s*. 6*d*. net.
THE HOUSE BY THE RIVER. 3*s*. 6*d*. net.

HOLDSWORTH (Sir W. S.).

A HISTORY OF ENGLISH LAW. In Nine Volumes. £1 5*s*. net each.
INDEX VOLUME. £1 1*s*. net.

HUTTON (Edward).

CITIES OF SICILY. Illustrated. 10*s*. 6*d*. net.
MILAN AND LOMBARDY.
THE CITIES OF ROMAGNA AND THE MARCHES.
SIENA AND SOUTHERN TUSCANY. NAPLES AND SOUTHERN ITALY.
Each illustrated. 8*s*. 6*d*. net.
THE CITIES OF UMBRIA. THE CITIES OF SPAIN.
VENICE AND VENETIA. A WAYFARER IN UNKNOWN TUSCANY.
FLORENCE AND NORTHERN TUSCANY. ROME.
COUNTRY WALKS ABOUT FLORENCE.
Each illustrated. 7*s*. 6*d*. net.

INGE (W. R.), Dean of St. Paul's.

CHRISTIAN MYSTICISM. 7*s*. 6*d*. net.

JOHNS (Rowland).

LET'S TALK OF DOGS. LUCKY DOGS.
PUPPIES.
Each illustrated. 6*s*. net.
DOGS YOU'D LIKE TO MEET. LET DOGS DELIGHT.
ALL SORTS OF DOGS.
Each illustrated. 3*s*. 6*d*. net.

"OUR FRIEND THE DOG" SERIES. Edited by ROWLAND JOHNS. Six Volumes:
THE CAIRN. THE PEKINGESE.
THE COCKER SPANIEL. THE AIREDALE.
THE FOX-TERRIER. THE ALSATIAN.
Each 2*s*. 6*d*. net.

KENDRICK (T. D.).

A HISTORY OF THE VIKINGS. Illustrated. 18*s*. net.
THE AXE AGE. Illustrated. 6*s*. net.
THE DRUIDS. Illustrated. 12*s*. 6*d*. net.
THE ARCHAEOLOGY OF THE CHANNEL ISLANDS. Vol. I. The Bailiwick of Guernsey. Illustrated. £1 5*s*. net.

KIPLING (Rudyard).

BARRACK-ROOM BALLADS. THE SEVEN SEAS.
THE FIVE NATIONS. DEPARTMENTAL DITTIES.
THE YEARS BETWEEN.

Four Editions of these famous volumes of poems are now issued, viz.: Crown 8vo, Buckram, 7*s*. 6*d*. net. F'cap 8vo, Cloth, 6*s*. net. Leather, 7*s*. 6*d*. net. Service Edition.—Two vols. each book. Square F'cap 8vo, 3*s*. net. each vol.

TWENTY POEMS. 1*s*. net.
A CHOICE OF SONGS. 2*s*. net.
SELECTED POEMS. 1*s*. net.
A KIPLING ANTHOLOGY—VERSE. Cloth, 6*s*. net and 3*s*. 6*d*. net. Leather, 7*s*. 6*d*. net.

KNOX (E. V.) ("Evoe").

SLIGHT IRRITATIONS. PARODIES REGAINED.
FOLLY CALLING.
Each 5*s*. net.

THESE LIBERTIES. 4*s*. 6*d*. net.

FANCY NOW! FICTION AS SHE IS WROTE
MR. PUNCH ON THE LINKS.
Each 6*s*. net.

AWFUL OCCASIONS. GORGEOUS TIMES.
IT OCCURS TO ME. WONDERFUL OUTINGS.
THIS OTHER EDEN. HERE'S MISERY!
THINGS THAT ANNOY ME. QUAINT SPECIMENS.
Each 3*s*. 6*d*. net.

LAMB (Charles and Mary).

THE COMPLETE WORKS. Edited by E. V. LUCAS. Six Volumes. 6*s*. net each. The volumes are:

1. MISCELLANEOUS PROSE.
2. ELIA AND THE LAST ESSAYS OF ELIA.
3. BOOKS FOR CHILDREN.
4. PLAYS AND POEMS.
5 and 6. LETTERS.

SELECTED LETTERS. Edited by G. T. CLAPTON. 3*s*. 6*d*. net.
THE CHARLES LAMB DAY BOOK. Compiled by E. V. LUCAS. 6*s*. net.

LANKESTER (Sir Ray).

SCIENCE FROM AN EASY CHAIR.
SCIENCE FROM AN EASY CHAIR (Second Series).
DIVERSIONS OF A NATURALIST. GREAT AND SMALL THINGS.
Each illustrated. 7*s*. 6*d*. net.

SECRETS OF EARTH AND SEA. Illustrated. 8*s*. 6*d*. net.

LAUGHLIN (Clara E.).

SO YOU'RE GOING TO GERMANY AND AUSTRIA!
SO YOU'RE GOING TO SPAIN! SO YOU'RE GOING TO FRANCE!
SO YOU'RE GOING TO PARIS! SO YOU'RE GOING TO ROME!
SO YOU'RE GOING TO ITALY! SO YOU'RE GOING TO ENGLAND!
Each illustrated. 10*s*. 6*d*. net.

LINDRUM (Walter).

BILLIARDS. Illustrated. 6*s*. net.

LODGE (Sir Oliver).

MAN AND THE UNIVERSE. 7*s*. 6*d*. net and 3*s*. 6*d*. net.
THE SURVIVAL OF MAN. 7*s*. 6*d*. net.
RAYMOND. 10*s*. 6*d*. net.
RAYMOND REVISED. 6*s*. net.
MODERN PROBLEMS. 3*s*. 6*d*. net.
REASON AND BELIEF. 3*s*. 6*d*. net.
THE SUBSTANCE OF FAITH. 2*s*. net.
RELATIVITY. 1*s*. net.
CONVICTION OF SURVIVAL. 2*s*. net.

LUCAS (E. V.).

The Life of Charles Lamb. Two Volumes. £1 1*s.* net.
The Colvins and Their Friends. £1 1*s.* net.
Vermeer the Magical. 5*s.* net.
A Wanderer in Rome. 10*s.* 6*d.* net.
A Wanderer in Holland. 10*s.* 6*d.* net.
A Wanderer in London. 10*s.* 6*d.* net.
London Revisited (Revised). 10*s.* 6*d.* net.
A Wanderer in Paris. 10*s.* 6*d.* net.
A Wanderer in Florence. 10*s.* 6*d.* net.
A Wanderer in Venice. 10*s.* 6*d.* net.
A Wanderer Among Pictures. 8*s.* 6*d.* net.
E. V. Lucas's London. £1 net.
The Open Road. 6*s.* net. India Paper, Leather, 7*s.* 6*d.* net.
Illustrated by Claude A. Shepperson. 10*s.* 6*d.* net.
The Joy of Life. Cloth. 6*s.* net.
Leather, 7*s.* 6*d.* net. India Paper, Leather, 7*s.* 6*d.* net.

Fireside and Sunshine.
Character and Comedy.
One Day and Another.
Loiterer's Harvest.
Events and Embroideries.
The Gentlest Art.
Giving and Receiving.
Encounters and Diversions.
Traveller's Luck.
Advisory Ben.
The Second Post.
Good Company.
A Fronded Isle.
Old Lamps for New.
Luck of the Year.
A Rover I Would Be.
Her Infinite Variety.
Turning Things Over.
Windfall's Eve.
At the Sign of the Dove.

Each 3*s.* 6*d.* net.

The Phantom Journal.
Zigzags in France.
Visibility Good.

Each 6*s.* net.

The Barber's Clock. 5*s.* net.
French Leaves. Illustrated. 5*s.* net.

"The More I See of Men . . ."
Out of a Clear Sky.
If Dogs Could Write.
". . . And Such Small Deer."

Each 3*s.* 6*d.* net.

No-Nose at the Show. Illustrated. 2*s.* 6*d.* net.
The Pekinese National Anthem. Illustrated. 1*s.* net.
See also **Lamb** (C. and M.).

LYND (Robert).

The Blue Lion.
The Money-Box.
The Little Angel.
The Green Man.
The Peal of Bells.
The Orange Tree.
The Goldfish.
The Pleasures of Ignorance.
It's a Fine World.

Each 3*s.* 6*d.* net.

Rain, Rain, Go to Spain. 5*s.* net.

McDOUGALL (William).

An Introduction to Social Psychology. 10*s.* 6*d.* net.
Body and Mind. 12*s.* 6*d.* net.
An Outline of Psychology. 10*s.* 6*d.* net.
National Welfare and Decay. 6*s.* net.
Ethics and Some Modern World Problems. 7*s.* 6*d.* net.
An Outline of Abnormal Psychology. 15*s.* net.
Character and the Conduct of Life. 10*s.* 6*d.* net.
Modern Materialism and Emergent Evolution. 7*s.* 6*d.* net.
A Brief Outline of Psychology: Normal and Abnormal.
8*s.* 6*d.* net.

MAETERLINCK (Maurice).
THE BLUE BIRD. 6*s.* net and 2*s.* 6*d.* net.
THE BETROTHAL. 6*s.* net and 3*s.* 6*d.* net.
DEATH. 3*s.* 6*d.* net.
OUR ETERNITY. 6*s.* net.
THE UNKNOWN GUEST. 6*s.* net.

MALLET (Sir C. E.).
A HISTORY OF THE UNIVERSITY OF OXFORD. Three Volumes. Illustrated. Each £1 1*s.* net.

MARLOWE (Christopher).
The Works of. In 6 Vols. General Editor, R. H. CASE.
I. LIFE OF MARLOWE; AND DIDO, QUEEN OF CARTHAGE. 8*s.* 6*d.* net.
II. TAMBURLAINE THE GREAT. 10*s.* 6*d.* net.
III. THE JEW OF MALTA and THE MASSACRE AT PARIS. 10*s.* 6*d.* net.
IV. POEMS. 10*s.* 6*d.* net.
V. DR. FAUSTUS. 8*s.* 6*d.* net.
VI. EDWARD II. 10*s.* 6*d.* net.

METHUEN (Sir A.).
AN ANTHOLOGY OF MODERN VERSE.
SHAKESPEARE TO HARDY: An Anthology of English Lyrics.
Each, Cloth, 6*s.* net. Leather, 7*s.* 6*d.* net.

MILNE (A. A.).
THOSE WERE THE DAYS. 7*s.* 6*d.* net.
TOAD OF TOAD HALL. A Play from Kenneth Grahame's "THE WIND IN THE WILLOWS." 5*s.* net.
NOT THAT IT MATTERS.
IF I MAY.
THE DAY'S PLAY.
THE HOLIDAY ROUND.
ONCE A WEEK.
THE SUNNY SIDE.
BY WAY OF INTRODUCTION.
MR. PIM PASSES BY.
Each 3*s.* 6*d.* net.
WHEN WE WERE VERY YOUNG.
WINNIE-THE-POOH.
NOW WE ARE SIX.
THE HOUSE AT POOH CORNER.
Each illustrated by E. H. SHEPARD. 7*s.* 6*d.* net. Leather, 10*s.* 6*d.* net.
THE CHRISTOPHER ROBIN STORY BOOK. Illustrated by E. H. SHEPARD. 5*s.* net.
THE CHRISTOPHER ROBIN BIRTHDAY BOOK. Illustrated by E. H. SHEPARD. 3*s.* 6*d.* net.
FOR THE LUNCHEON INTERVAL. 1*s.* 6*d.* net.

MORTON (H. V.).
THE HEART OF LONDON. 3*s.* 6*d.* net. Also, Illustrated by L. HUMMEL. 6*s.* net.
THE SPELL OF LONDON.
THE NIGHTS OF LONDON.
Each 3*s.* 6*d.* net.
IN SEARCH OF ENGLAND.
THE CALL OF ENGLAND.
IN SEARCH OF SCOTLAND.
IN SEARCH OF IRELAND.
IN SEARCH OF WALES.
Each illustrated. 7*s.* 6*d.* net.

NORWOOD (Gilbert).
GREEK TRAGEDY.
GREEK COMEDY.
Each 12*s.* 6*d.* net.

PETRIE (Sir Flinders).
A HISTORY OF EGYPT. Illustrated. Six Volumes.
1. FROM THE IST TO XVITH DYNASTY (12*s.* net). 2. THE XVIITH AND XVIIITH DYNASTIES (9*s.* net). 3. XIXTH TO XXXTH DYNASTIES (12*s.* net). 4. PTOLEMAIC EGYPT. EDWYN BEVAN. (15*s.* net.) 5. EGYPT UNDER ROMAN RULE. J. G. MILNE. (12*s.* net.) 6. EGYPT IN THE MIDDLE AGES. STANLEY LANE-POOLE. (10*s.* net.)

RICHARDSON (T. D.).
MODERN FIGURE SKATING. Illustrated. 15*s.* net.

RUTTER (Frank).
El Greco. Illustrated. £1 10*s*. net.

SELLAR (W. C.) and YEATMAN (R. J.).
1066 and All That. A comic history. Illustrated by John Reynolds. 5*s*. net.

SOMERVELL (D. C.).
English Thought in the Nineteenth Century. 6*s*. net.

TILDEN (William T.).
The Art of Lawn Tennis (Revised Edition).
Singles and Doubles.
Each illustrated. 6*s*. net.
Lawn Tennis for Young Players.
Lawn Tennis for Club Players.
Lawn Tennis for Match Players.
Each illustrated. 2*s*. 6*d*. net
The Common Sense of Lawn Tennis.
Match Play and the Spin of the Ball.
Each illustrated. 5*s*. net.

UNDERHILL (Evelyn).
Mysticism. (Revised Edition.) 15*s*. net.
The Life of the Spirit and the Life of To-day. 7*s*. 6*d*. net.
Concerning the Inner Life. The House of the Soul.
Each 2*s*. net.
Man and the Supernatural. 7*s*. 6*d*. net.

VARDON (Harry).
How to Play Golf. Illustrated. 5*s*. net.
The Complete Golfer. Illustrated. 12*s*. 6*d*. net.

WARD (A. C.).
Twentieth-Century Literature. 5*s*. net.
The Nineteen-Twenties. 5*s*. net.
Landmarks in Western Literature. 5*s*. net.

WILDE (Oscar).
The Works of Oscar Wilde. Sixteen Volumes. Each 6*s*. 6*d*. net. Some also 2*s*. 6*d*. net.
1. Lord Arthur Savile's Crime and the Portrait of Mr. W. H. 2. The Duchess of Padua. 3. Poems. 4. Lady Windermere's Fan. 5. A Woman of no Importance. 6. An Ideal Husband. 7. The Importance of being Earnest. 8. A House of Pomegranates. 9. Intentions. 10. De Profundis and Prison Letters. 11. Essays. 12. Salome, A Florentine Tragedy, and La Sainte Courtisane. 14. Selected Prose of Oscar Wilde. 15. Art and Decoration. 16. For Love of the King: A Burmese Masque (5*s*. net). 17. Vera, or the Nihilists.

METHUEN'S HISTORY OF MEDIEVAL AND MODERN EUROPE

In 8 vols. Each 16*s*. net.

I. 476 to 911. By J. H. Baxter.
II. 911 to 1198. By Z. N. Brooke.
III. 1198 to 1378. By C. W. Previté-Orton.
IV. 1378 to 1494. By W. T. Waugh.
V. 1494 to 1610. By A. J. Grant.
VI. 1610 to 1715. By E. R. Adair.
VII. 1715 to 1815. By W. F. Reddaway.
VIII. 1815 to 1923. By Sir J. A. R. Marriott